T0059822

THE STARS
IN MY SKY

THE STARS IN MY SKY

Those who brightened my film journey

DIVYA DUTTA

Foreword by AMITABH BACHCHAN

EBURY
PRESS

An imprint of Penguin Random House

EBURY PRESS

USA | Canada | UK | Ireland | Australia
New Zealand | India | South Africa | China

Ebury Press is part of the Penguin Random House group of companies
whose addresses can be found at global.penguinrandomhouse.com

Published by Penguin Random House India Pvt. Ltd
4th Floor, Capital Tower 1, MG Road,
Gurugram 122 002, Haryana, India

Penguin
Random House
India

First published in Ebury Press by Penguin Random House India 2021

ISBN 9780670094196

Bhaag Milkha Bhaag film still courtesy Viacom 18 Media Private Limited.
Working still of the film *Badlapur* courtesy Maddock Films Private Limited ('Maddock').
The rest of the photographs are the author's own.

Typeset in Minion Pro by Manipal Technologies Limited, Manipal
Printed at Replika Press Pvt. Ltd, India

www.penguin.co.in

You know, Ma, I wouldn't have been an actor had you not had confidence in me and my dreams. Thanks for making me believe that dreams do come true!
This one is for you . . .

CONTENTS

Foreword   ix

Author's Note   xi

Amitabh Bachchan   1

Yash Chopra   15

Sonu Nigam   23

Shah Rukh Khan   33

Shyam Benegal   43

Juhi Chawla   57

Rakeysh Omprakash Mehra   63

Gulzar   77

Shabana Azmi   83

Neeraj Pandey   107

Dharmendra   121

Nitin Kakkar   127

Irrfan Khan   135

Salman Khan   147

Sriram Raghavan   155

Gurdas Maan   165

Rishi Kapoor   173

Jackie Shroff   179

Sonali Bendre   185

Javed Akhtar   193

Naseeruddin Shah   201

Raju Hirani   205

Anupam Kher   211

Rajit Kapur   215

Anubhav Sinha   223

Dev Anand   229

Aditya Chopra   233

Hrishikesh Mukherjee   243

Dilip Kumar   247

Prem Chopra   251

Vinod Khanna   255

Deepak Bahry   257

Acknowledgements   261

FOREWORD

Divya Dutta writes her second book *The Stars in My Sky* and enumerates her various experiences with the people she worked with and how they impacted her journey, in her career in the film industry.

That she is on to another book merely demonstrates her insatiable desire to connect her experiences with the world of her creativity; a creativity that has been as insatiable as her desire to write.

Her varied performances in the list of her films have ever proved that she is beyond being an accomplished artist; she has lived to the very core of each character that she has so meaningfully carved.

It was my great privilege to have been in her company in front of the camera, and I do look forward to meeting her again in this new venture of hers.

My very best wishes to her and may she continue to enchant us with her most impactful presence.

Mumbai   Amitabh Bachchan
3 September 2021

AUTHOR'S NOTE

I have realized two professions are the most amazing! Acting and writing . . . they both allow you to express yourself as a part of your job . . . in fact, that is the basic requirement.

Fortunately, I chose acting as my profession. Playing varied roles . . . getting an opportunity to live a few real and some fictional characters; becoming them . . . feeling them and in those few months of playing them, expressing emotions as they would and not as me, Divya. Isn't it intriguing? Well, I feel lucky . . . that I live and experience life not just as me . . . but in the process of playing others, I also get to experience theirs! The *ek ke saath ek muft* scheme is always dear. Here, in just one life, I get to experience many! Being an actor. An absolute bonanza.

As far as writing goes, I started with weekly columns in newspapers . . . initially just for the heck of it, but I gradually realized that people were connecting with my writing. They identified with my stories; they could relate to my experiences.

I distinctly remember this one time when I had gone to perform a play in Delhi. After the show, an old lady came up on stage and hugged me tight (a blissful feeling from the pre-COVID days). I obviously thought it was for my performance . . .

but she whispered, 'You, of course, perform fabulously but I have a connect with you through your columns. I have to thank you for motivating me to be my own best friend through one of your write-ups! For the first time in my life, I travelled alone at the age of sixty-five on a solo holiday, thanks to you. I didn't wait for ever for my husband or sons to take me! I have to thank you for that experience, *beta*!'

I never forgot that. And after that, I never stopped writing. I loved this additional connect I had with the people, as my audience and as readers!

My first book, *Me and Ma,* happened at jet speed. It was like someone up there had the script ready and we just had to go on the floor. I was facing my worst fear, that of losing my Ma. I was dazed . . . numb . . . there were too many feelings. But the biggest was of gratitude towards her for being mine. I wanted to celebrate the rock star that she was. It seemed like she had planned it all for me already. I knew what the title of the book would be before I had the first chapter in place. It was to be called *Me and Ma*. I knew instinctively that I wanted it to be published with Penguin Random House and my editor Vaishali Mathur was godsent. She heard the synopsis and responded with a warm, instant yes. I didn't even realize when I had finished writing it . . . it was catharsis . . . and the book reached where it had to, right into people's hearts. The best feeling was when readers called or met me and said, 'The first thing we did after reading your book was to go and hug our mom,' and that was truly gratifying!

That book introduced me to another world. The world of writers and authors . . . of festivals and seminars . . . and I really started loving this different feeling of being an author! My new profile was actor/author. And I was absorbing and cherishing every moment of it.

Strangely and fortunately, no one ever thought I was a one-book wonder! Whoever I met asked, 'So, when is your next book coming and what is it about?' The question followed me everywhere.

And then I finally confronted it. What next? What was it that I was extremely passionate about? I could only think of one thing—movies. My journey as an actor; a journey sans any godfather . . . of a girl from a small town, coming from a family of doctors, to realize her dreams with no backing and zero experience. All I had was my lovely mom to support me and believe in me and my crazy passion to be an actor. Just that. Nothing else.

From being someone who started with multi-starrers as a cute something with two songs and two romantic scenes to now working with the who's who of the industry with roles written for me, these twenty-five years of being in a place I absolutely adore, have been embedded in my heart. And what made it even more special were the few people I met during this journey, who have impacted my life in their own unassuming ways. They left a mark; held my hand to help me jump across that little pit I was scared of crossing. I learnt a lot from merely observing how they faced their life's situations. Their subtle yet beautiful presence in my life changed something inside me . . . made me a new person . . . every day.

Even now, when I think of them, a broad smile spreads on my face . . . for the cheer they brought me; the strength, love and warmth they gave me and their unshakeable belief in me.

This book is for them . . . about them.

This book is to celebrate those whose work I grew up watching. And they are now an integral part of my life and some—my peers and colleagues and directors—who, when I look back, have held my hand when I stumbled . . . patted my back and said, 'Heyyy, run! The field is yours!' Sometimes, that's all one needs!

And sometimes, it's important to let them know what they mean to you.

So here I am, sharing another piece of my heart with you all. It comprises my experiences with all these super talented people I truly love and admire. It is my little way of saying thank you for all those precious moments. Thank you for being there and thank you for being YOU.

You are the stars in my sky.

AMITABH BACHCHAN

I was jumping on my bed with sheer excitement. In the lows of the lockdown, it seemed ironical, but I had a reason. I had just read a message, and it was very special. That message was from someone who was the reason I, like many others, had joined the film industry. That message was from someone I dote on, someone who's a legend, someone who was an integral part of my childhood. And now, I have a special bond with him. Life does find ways to fulfil your dreams, this being the biggest of them all—to be like him, to share screen space with him and to know him—that dream is now beautifully realized, and I'm all gratitude.

It all started when I was four . . . I had just come back from watching an amazing film, *Mr Natwarlal*, with my aunt. The little me had been completely enamoured by that tall gentleman, dancing so gracefully to *'Mere Paas Aao Mere Doston'*. I had felt like I was one of the *dosts*, and he was singing just for me, so I was super attentive to all that he did on screen. I had clapped throughout the film, and asked my aunt the name of the handsome hero. 'Amitabh Bachchan,' she quipped with

equal excitement. I guessed he was a favourite with all, and I
had joined that list of his admirers too.

From then on, I would watch all his movies. I would come
back home and try to dance like him. After *Laawaris*, I think
everyone in my school and all the neighbourhood kids knew of
my adulation for him.

I remember clearly—once after school—I had organized
a dance performance on my veranda. There was a huge
cement bench there which served as my stage. I'd invited the
neighbourhood kids to come spend an evening of entertainment
(such was my belief!) with me, with the promise that they
would be served hot gulab jamuns and jalebis while enjoying
the performance.

The preparations had been done. I had taken Ma's red
dupatta and tied it around my waist. Dad's white shirt, which
reached my toes and beyond, was my kurta. I had applied Ma's
lipstick, symbolizing red paan stains, as I wasn't allowed to
have paan. Ma's sarees were used to decorate the background.
The music was ready, and so was my audience—with paper
plates full of chips, samosas and gulab jamuns. If they liked
my performance and clapped, Rooh Afza was kept handy as an
additional treat.

I performed to '*Khaike Paan Banaras Wallah*'. And as the
music played, all I could remember was Amitabh Bachchan,
the way he danced, the way he smiled, and the way he chewed
that paan. Before I knew it, the song was over and so was my
performance. I had enjoyed it so much, while being absolutely
immersed in his world. How I would have loved to do just that
all my life! There was applause. And yes, Rooh Afza was served.

After a few days, preparations for the school's annual
function began. To my dismay, I was offered the role of a
background dancer dressed in a flower costume, and all I had

to do was sway! I hated it! I wanted to perform! I wanted to take centre stage. I wanted the audience to watch me!

Miraculously, someone up there had heard my heartfelt desire.

Unfortunately (well . . .), the child playing the lead got fever just two days before the annual function. The teacher rushed into our class and asked, 'Does anyone know how to dance like Amitabh Bachchan?' Without batting an eyelid, everyone looked at me.

Now I was on centre stage as the protagonist! My mother was in the audience, sitting with my class teacher who didn't know then that she was my mother. She whispered in my mother's ear, 'Watch this girl who'll come now, she's very good! A natural with Bachchan steps!' Ma was glowing with sheer pride.

On the stage, I had been transported into that magical world of Amitabh Bachchan again. I danced as I visualized him on the big screen, and felt a surge of sheer joy. I performed as if in a trance and then slowly, I could hear something in the distance. I was transported back from my reverie by sounds of applause and the sound of cheers. Yes, that was my audience, and I bowed to them. While bowing, I stared at the stage under my feet and then looked at the happy audience. I was ecstatic! Yes! This was where I belonged. This was my calling. I didn't know then how it would be fulfilled, but I knew I wanted it definitely. I wanted to belong to that big screen that had shown me the magic of Amitabh Bachchan.

Years later, when I was selected to be part of the *Stardust Talent Hunt*, we were rehearsing a scene at the bungalow in Madh Island where all of us were put up. And that's when our teacher came and broke the news. We had a special guest coming to visit us. Yes, Mr Amitabh Bachchan! He had been kind enough to agree to come and meet us. I was elated and, it goes without saying, couldn't sleep all night. I just couldn't wait for the morning!

I was the first to be up and about. I selected my favourite dress and rehearsed (no, not the scene but what I would say to him) a few hundred times. At dot 11 a.m., he arrived. I had heard he was extremely punctual. And he was. As he entered the room, everyone surrounded him in awe. He met each student patiently and warmly, and I was eagerly waiting for my turn. I tried to move towards him, but my feet were stuck to the ground. I was too mesmerized by what was happening in front of me. I was pinching myself to move, but was unable to, until I heard my teacher call out. '*Arey*, come here and meet sir. Why are you standing behind?'

I walked up to him as if on autopilot mode. I wasn't sure if I should have shaken hands with him or greeted him with a namaste. I ended up doing a mix of both. Then I heard that baritone voice for real for the first time. 'Hello, I'm Amitabh Bachchan.' I stood awestruck. *Did he have to introduce himself?* I felt so important and relevant. Yes, he has the knack of making the other person feel very comfortable. There was a slight smile on his face, but his eyes seemed to observe everything. I'm sure nothing was missed, not even my trembling hands and the nervous smile. Of course, I had forgotten all I had mugged up. All that came out was, 'Hi, I'm Divya Dutta, sir!' If he was amused, he didn't show it.

He left after spending some time with all of us. Everyone had tried to make conversation with him, but I hadn't spoken another word. I was only observing and absorbing.

Later, of course, I was very irritated with myself for not living up to my own expectations. This was blasphemous—I mean, to meet Mr Bachchan for the first time and stand there like a statue was unpardonable. God only knew when I'd see him again or even get the opportunity to do so.

My friends started pulling my leg. '*Iski toh bolti band ho gayi!* (She was speechless!)' I was sad, I just wished I could get another chance to meet him, and then I'd talk with him. Lots. *Jee bhar ke.*

I really wished for it, and it happened.

My third film was *Baghban*. I was told my role was that of a nasty daughter-in-law, and I was going to share most of my screen space with Mr Bachchan. It goes without saying that I signed on the dotted line without hesitation. I called up Ma, and gave her the good news. This surely was a dream come true! She understood my excitement. She had seen me live with that dream, and it was finally going to come true.

Shooting was to start on the day of the mahurat itself.

I had reached much before my call time to be absolutely ready for my first scene with Mr Bachchan. Oh my god! What had I just said? My first scene with Mr Bachchan! Yes, it was finally turning into a reality. The megastar was the reason I had been motivated to be in the movies. And now, I would be acting alongside him. As soon as I was called to join the mahurat shot, I literally ran, hoping the assistant director hadn't noticed my overenthusiasm and excitement. I didn't want to miss even a second of this huge day. The set was buzzing with activity and full of people, all busy making arrangements before Mr Bachchan arrived.

Suddenly, there was pin-drop silence, and everyone looked in one direction: the entrance. At 10 a.m. sharp, Mr Bachchan arrived. Those who were sitting, instinctively got up. Those who were standing, straightened up. That is the charisma of Amitabh Bachchan. Everyone was waiting to say hello to him. He, looking majestic in his attire, standing tall amongst the rest of the gathering, patiently and warmly met everyone. And then came my turn. And I did a repeat. I barely managed a 'Good morning, sir!' Again, I was annoyed with myself for not adding a few more conversational lines.

The mahurat shot was taken with him, the lovely Hema Malini and us. And then, the shoot began. The scene that we began with was me shouting at my child for helping his grandfather, Mr Bachchan, with his new spectacles. We all sat for rehearsals with our director, the very warm and affable, late Ravi Chopra. Mr Bachchan sat right in front of me. I couldn't take my eyes off him while he read his lines. He was absolutely in character even during the rehearsal and every time he read the lines, he did it a new way for the director to choose which tone he liked best. Not once did Mr Bachchan say, 'Come on, let's just shoot now.' He sat there patiently, rehearsing with us newcomers until the director said, 'Okay, let's take it.'

I was amazed by his discipline, his calmness and dedication. For me, that scene shall always be special. My first shot with my most favourite of them all (it is sad that I could never express it enough to him).

A few days went by. Everything seemed to go well. I had still not progressed beyond 'Hi, how are you, sir?' but there was always a very bright and happy 'Very good morning, sir' that came straight from my heart.

One day, I came back home from the shoot and as soon as Ma asked me, 'How are you?', I burst into tears. She was taken aback. 'What happened? Did the scene not go well or are you not well?' But the scene had gone off well and I was well too, physically at least.

What I hadn't realized that time was that somewhere, I had been hugely affected by the scenes where I had been nasty to Amit ji . . . I had done those scenes well, but subconsciously, they had had an impact on me. The man who was my favourite, the man whom I wanted to tell all about how much I looked up to him and adored him, but just couldn't muster enough courage to do so. I was actually mouthing mean lines to him, feeling terrible inside and not realizing it. It was clear, that as a new actor, I just didn't know how to disconnect from my role after the shoot. I was feeling horrible about being irreverent and obnoxious (even if it was only on screen) to the man I adored the most.

The next day, I went to the shoot with a heavy heart. By then, I had had enough of not being nice to Mr Bachchan. I didn't want to say those lines and see his helpless face. My heart bled. I had no choice but to play my role. Unwillingly (very unlike me), I went to the set, forced a happy expression to say hello to Amit ji, rehearsed the mean lines in the scene, and controlled myself from crying again.

With so much happening, however, I hadn't realized that someone was observing it all. He had seen my happy, chirpy good mornings to him every day. But that day, he saw me in a different avatar, all upset. The sensitive person in him had caught my problem immediately, but he made no fuss about it. He dealt with it in a very smart way. He called me to sit next to him. I was a bit surprised, but obviously happy. Then, when I sat next to him, he said, '*Divya ji, aap jo hain na, humse bahut bura behave kar rahi hain* (You are behaving very badly with me).'

I instinctively answered defensively, 'No, sir, never in my wildest dreams. *Yeh toh role hai!*' I hadn't realized until then that what I had just said was what I needed to understand myself! And he had effortlessly driven home the point.

He continued mischievously, '*Aur nahi toh kya. Itna daant rahi hain aap humein. Aur hamara role angry man ka toh hai nahin, isliye hamare fans jo hain, wo hockey le ke peeche padh jayenge aapke* (It is true. You are scolding me so much. My role is not that of an angry young man. My fans will come after you with a hockey stick).'

Continuing this leg-pulling, he called his man Friday, and asked for his hockey stick, '*Suno, meri hockey (stick) lao.*' He picked up that hockey stick and acted out how the audience would react on seeing me being mean to him. Everyone on the set started laughing. I didn't even realize when a smile touched the corners of my lips. How beautifully he had made me realize what was bothering me without even mentioning that he was aware of it, somewhere subconsciously putting it in my head that it was just a role and not to be taken so seriously.

He laughed too, and said, '*Gajak khayengi aap? Khaas Allahabad se ayi hai* (Will you have some sweets? They've come especially from Allahabad).' His man Friday placed a huge dabba full of a variety of sweets made from jaggery and nuts in front of me. I was being pampered. I was being soothed, without even realizing it, by this ultra-sensitive and observant superstar. He really didn't have to. But what amazes me is that not only was he sensitive to a newcomer's inner turmoil, but also helped me out of it. I was back to my happy, chirpy self.

Now, I mustered up the courage to slowly pull my chair close to his and sit with him without feeling guilty about being mean. Thanks to him, I had learnt to disconnect from my role. Thanks to him, I could deal with the role professionally, without getting carried away by it.

But his straight-faced jokes continued, always teaching me something. I remember once when we were shooting at an outdoor location and my man Friday brought me a glass of water. I drank it right away. Mr Bachchan immediately quipped, '*Arey, pani pi rahi hain aap, aur humein poocha bhi nahi? Humein bhi toh pyaas lagi hai* (You are drinking water, but you didn't even ask me if I wanted some. I'm thirsty too).' He was joking, of course, but after that day I have never had water before asking others.

The movie wrapped up and life moved on. One fine day, I got a call from an unknown number.

'Hi, yes?' I said casually.

'Hi, Divya!' I instantly stood up on hearing that baritone voice. 'Amitabh Bachchan here,' he said.

'Yes, sir. Ji, of course, sir,' I mumbled as I straightened up.

'We have a Holi celebration, and it would be great if you could join us,' he said.

Wow, really? Mr Bachchan had personally called to invite me. 'Ji, sir. I will surely come!'

How humble! How warmly he had invited me! I loosened up when he hung up and jumped on the bed a few times before calling my mother to share my excitement.

Clad in all-white attire, I reached the gates of his famous landmark bungalow, Prateeksha. I had passed by many times, always seeing crowds of people waiting to catch a glimpse of Big B. He would also reciprocate their adulation by making an appearance to greet his fans. That day, I actually got into that iconic bungalow.

Mr Bachchan and Abhishek (who I met for the first time that day), greeted me graciously and welcomed me inside. But before I could even absorb my surroundings, I was picked up and dunked into a pool of colours, with a 'Happy Holi!' from all sides. That day, the colours of Holi shone brighter for me than ever before. That day was my most special Holi, celebrated with the most gracious of hosts, the Bachchans.

On paper, I did three more films with Mr Bachchan—*Veer-Zaara, Delhi-6* and *The Last Lear*. I shared only one shot with him in *The Last Lear*. In the others, we didn't have any scenes together.

Arjun Rampal and I went to Kolkata with Mr Bachchan for a press conference for *The Last Lear*. The huge mall, which was the venue, was packed with people right up to the top floor to see their *damaad babu*. It was a sight to behold, to see so much love being bestowed on the man who had epitomized excellence in an unparalleled manner. His is an inspiring story, absolutely! From *Saat Hindustani* to *Zanjeer*, from *Sholay* to *Kabhi Kabhie*, from *Chupke Chupke* to *Deewar*, and then from *Pink*, *Piku*, *Paa* to *Gulabo Sitabo,* there isn't a role he hasn't played and that too with brilliance. There's not a story that is thought of, without him in it as the first choice. He is an institution in himself, someone who stood tall in a career spanning a good fifty years, always at the top of his craft.

At another press conference in Delhi, he said something that took me by surprise, and left me elated. As one of the journalists asked him who his favourite actress was, he said after a pause, '*Hamare ghar mein, khaas taur pe hamari patni Jaya, Divya ko bahut pasand kiya jata hai* (In my home, all of us, especially my wife Jaya, like Divya a lot).' That statement was like a blessing from the universe; that line completed the huge circle of my life. From my beginnings, dancing to Mr Bachchan's songs as a child, and aspiring to be like him, to being with him in the same frame and then to hear this from him when he was seated next to me, meant and continues to mean the world to me.

I shut my eyes for a few seconds. I didn't want that tear to fall. But when I did open my eyes, I had the brightest smile ever.

From then on, I've met sir once a year for sure, at his very famous Diwali parties. In spite of the entire industry's who's who being present there, the Bachchans make sure that everyone is welcomed and seen off personally, and very well taken care of. During one such party, he welcomed me with, '*Suniye devi ji, Bhaag Milkha Bhaag dekhi. Itna badhiya kaise kar leti hain?* (I watched *Bhaag Milkha Bhaag*. Please tell me how do you manage to do your roles so well?)'

Coming from him, who very humbly concentrates on making the guest feel welcome and comfortable, it was the most beautiful takeaway for me.

Mr Bachchan has the sweetest habit of wishing those close to him and his colleagues on their birthdays exactly at midnight.

The first time it happened, I was with my family and friends, and at sharp 12 a.m., I received a message from him. I read it and then reread it many times. Then, I slowly absorbed the words and jumped with joy. I looked in the mirror and bragged, '*Madam, suna hai Bachchan saab ne birthday wish kiya aapko! Wah. Kya baat!* (I've heard you've been wished by Bachchan saab! What an achievement!)' And I jumped up, clapping my hands together again.

I wish he knew how much joy he had brought this petite woman by his very thoughtful gesture. Now, after all these years, I wait for the clock to strike twelve on my birthday and look forward to reading his message.

After I wrote *Me and Ma*, I was sitting with my brother, Rahul, to plan the launch of this very special book. He said, 'If you had your way, who would you want to invite to launch your book?'

I said without even blinking, 'It will be a dream come true if Mr Amitabh Bachchan launches my first book, but . . .' I left the line unfinished. Rahul completed it for me, '. . . but what? You know him well. Pick up the phone and message him. I'm sure it will be positive. You must try your best for what you really want, na?'

It took me a day to muster up the courage to message Mr Bachchan, but when I wrote to him finally, it was all heart.

I knew how much it would mean to me to have him launch *Me and Ma*. After messaging him, the only thing I could do that day was keep looking at my mobile for a message to pop up. I could not focus on anything else. My heart had been beating fast all day—what if he declined?

In the evening, the mobile finally beeped with his name flashing on it. It was like an exam result. I took a few seconds before opening up the message. It said, 'Let me know the date and time you are looking at.' He had, again, been generous and said yes!

My first book was blessed. Everything that I had wanted for it had been happening smoothly but this was a feeling I'd never be able to explain. Suffice it to say that after he agreed, I just sat in my prayer room after very long (after Ma, I had stopped praying), and folded my hands in gratitude. Amitabh Bachchan had given his consent! It would be a dream launch for my book on my Ma.

I didn't sleep at all the night before the day of the launch. My day went in looking after the arrangements, and coordinating with everyone. Juhi Chawla and Sonali Bendre were going to read excerpts from the book, and Mr Bachchan had promised to come at 7.30 p.m. And of course, everyone knew he was supremely punctual.

Finally, everything seemed to be in place. Guests were arriving; the stage was set. I was called out to get some pictures clicked in the lobby. It was 7.15 p.m. There were still fifteen minutes for sir to arrive, I thought. As I was posing for the cameras, at a distance, I saw a lot of people surrounding someone. I saw a figure, patiently and humbly standing and waiting for me to finish what I was doing. I froze. Was it him? Yess!! It was him!

I instantly dropped what I was doing and ran to greet him. The sheer humility of the legend who gestured to me to carry on and complete what I was doing, as he was five minutes early! Would anything even look important enough in front of the megastar who stood next to me? At that point, he looked so endearing! I went and hugged him to greet him instead of my usual namaste. I was overwhelmed, big time!

He gently bent down to my five-foot-something frame to understand the flow of the event. I wish I could express what I was feeling at that time. I was releasing my Ma's book out to the world that day, and all my loved ones and the entire film clan were out in full support; each and every one of them was there with me at that moment. And then I had him, standing there with the most adorably innocent expression on his face, as if asking me, 'Tell me what you want me to do.'

I came out of my reverie and escorted him to the stage. Ma's book was launched with great fanfare, exactly like I wanted. And then, there was pin-drop silence when Mr Bachchan made his speech. I was pleasantly surprised that he had mentioned minute details from the book and about Ma. It seemed as though he had known her for a long time. And then, he warmly wished me good luck. I had a genuine smile on my face after very long that day. Ma probably was sitting somewhere amidst us and smiling too. This was a dream day, for me especially, and I had this one man to thank for it, but no words will ever be enough.

Cut to the lockdown. As I jumped in ecstasy, I looked at the mobile again, and read the message that had just flashed. I had shared my poem with Mr Bachchan for feedback. He stumped me with his humility and grace once again by writing back, '*Padhi. Achi lagi. Agar aapki ijaazat ho toh Twitter pe share karun?* (Read it. Liked it. If you permit, I would like to share it on Twitter).'

What had he just said? Was he asking me? I was on cloud nine! It was a huge deal anyway that he wanted to post my poem, and then he was humbly asking me if he could.

Well, they don't make them like you any more!

You, sir, mean more to me than I can ever express. You, sir, are the reason I am in the movies. I am lucky to not just have been on-screen with you, but to also have shared these gems of moments with my most favourite star as memories for life. Memories that make me smile broadly and make me jump on my bed with sheer joy.

The beautiful journey continues. I am honoured that I live in your time to experience your magic unfold on all media—the big screen, small screen, social media, ads and more. When it's you, it is super special.

As for me, I still am that little child who wore Ma's dupattas to dance like you, to be in the movies, just like you.

I am fortunate that today, I earn my living doing just that, belonging to the magical world of Amitabh Bachchan.

YASH CHOPRA

He was one of the main reasons why I wanted to be an actress, or rather, a heroine. The way he presented his heroines was nothing short of a dream. All the actresses looked their best in his films, inevitably also delivering the best performance of their career.

My reason for loving his movies was more than just his heroines. It was his films; the presentation, and his storytelling. I loved his movies—from *Kabhi Kabhie* to *Trishul*, and *Kaala Patthar* to *Lamhe* and *Chandni*—all of them. He had the ability to transport you to his world of love, romance, friendships, a certain complexity of relationships, and grandeur and beauty that one could only fantasize about. Be it the dynamics between Amitabh Bachchan, Waheeda Rehman, Rakhee ji and Shashi Kapoor in *Kabhi Kabhie*—especially the scene where both men profess their love for Rakhee ji; the complicated status of love in *Lamhe* or the sheer beauty and sensitive portrayal of Chandni and her pure love as pristine as the whites Sridevi wore in the film. Every film was unique and yet, it made you fall in love— with the story, with the cast, and . . . with cinema.

One would be considered at the top of the league if they were in a Yash Chopra film. All the big stars wanted to be featured in his films. If a newcomer was launched by him, it was a given that the industry was getting its new heart-throb.

For me, he was someone who understood relationships like no one else did and presented them sensitively in his distinct style.

Yes, I daydreamed during my college days—of being discovered by Yash Chopra; being launched opposite a big star and becoming the next Bollywood sensation. Whenever I would read of a new girl being launched by Yash ji in a film magazine, I would inevitably slip into dream mode and imagine myself as the next! I do think that when you really want something from the bottom of your heart, in whatever form and whichever way, the universe conspires to give it to you.

When I got selected in the talent hunt organized by *Stardust* magazine, I was called to Mumbai for the final round of selections. It was to be a performance in front of a panel of industry stalwarts. I had come to Mumbai with my mother, while no one else in the family was even aware of it. This was my only opportunity to follow my dream and I had to give it my all. If it didn't work out, I'd have to go back to Punjab and do something that was expected of me, like studying further, taking the civil services exam and eventually, getting married. This talent hunt was that one ray of hope that had actually brought me to Mumbai. Fate had handed me an opportunity of a lifetime.

Mom sat holding my hand and mumbling her prayers. As my name was announced, Ma wished me luck and this time, she said it out loud, 'Go, make your dream come true.'

The selections were happening at a five-star hotel in Juhu. I froze as I entered the room where I had been ushered in. Right in front of me sat the who's who of the industry—Subhash Ghai, Shekhar Kapur, Sooraj Barjatya and the man who I'd recognize anywhere (as it was my heart's desire to be discovered by him). Yash Chopra sat right in the middle. My legs felt like jelly. He was no longer just a dream. He was sitting before me—in reality. From a distance, I felt like he was asking me to start.

I managed to greet everyone. Then I told myself, 'You've got to give it your best; you've got to get them to take notice! This is your only chance!' I performed despite my nervousness, and, after finishing, in spite of my wobbly legs, I mustered a thank you. Before I left the room, I turned and looked at Yash ji again. *'OMG! I had actually seen him in person and performed in front of him too!'*

Selected or not, at least my wish to meet him had been fulfilled and I was grateful that I had at least come this far.

As luck would have it, I was among the chosen winners and my journey in the movies began, albeit in multi-starrers, and not in a Yash Chopra film (much to my dismay). But I learnt to make the best of opportunities that came my way in those years.

Once, while shooting in London, I received a call that Yash Chopra and Aditya Chopra would like to meet me. Post that, I had sleepless nights until I came back and fixed up the meeting. I had gone loony imagining and reimagining headlines like, 'Yash Chopra relaunches Divya Dutta'. I was sure I had hit the jackpot.

On the day of my appointment with Yash ji, I chose to wear a pristine white salwar kameez. When I reached the office, my heart was racing. I entered his office, and he met me very pleasantly. I sat on the other side of the table and kept pinching myself. Yesss!! I was with Yash Chopra; sitting right opposite him and he had called me for his next film! Could it get any better!

After exchanging pleasantries, he came straight to the point. 'So, I am making this film called *Veer-Zaara* which is written by Aditya (Chopra), and has Shah Rukh, Preity, Rani, Amitabh Bachchan and Hema Malini in it.'

I stiffened up. *What lead role could I possibly have with such a huge cast already in place?* Then I heard him say, 'I want you to play Preity's friend, Shabbo!'

I tied up my white dupatta in a few knots as thoughts raced in my head. I thought, '. . . the heroine's friend? In a Yash Chopra film? Hadn't he noticed that I had come dressed in white?' I was hoping, he'd say, 'I am joking! It is the lead role that I am offering you, opposite Shah Rukh.' But nothing of that sort happened. I was jolted back to reality. Finally, my dream of working with Yash ji was coming true but not in the way I had thought it would. Right then, Aditya (of whom I have spoken in his chapter) entered. After my narration with him and a great conversation, I was elated to take on Shabbo's role with all my heart. As I left, Yash ji came to see me off and said, 'Shabbo will be special.'

Preparations for Shabbo started in full swing. My look tests took place in a grand way. I was ushered into a huge room at the Yash Raj office where '*The* Manish Malhotra' had kept all my outfits ready. Yash ji was there in person to see what suited me best. Little things were added. The prints, patterns and colours to be used in each scene were discussed and I just looked on, amazed!

So that's how much work went into the look of a character!

My dialogue rehearsals were going on separately with Aditya Chopra.

And finally, the day of the shoot arrived. It was the first day of shooting for the film too. A large set of Preity's house in the film was erected in Film City. The first scene, to add to my nervousness, was a long monologue where I open all the curtains in the room and try to wake up Zaara. There was too much on my plate that day—the pressure of the first day of shoot, my lengthy monologue, and then the dialect that I was supposed to speak in. Additionally, the shoot was in sync sound mode (which meant no dubbing unless required) so I had to make sure my dialogue delivery in that dialect was articulate. To top it all, was the presence of Aditya Chopra and Shah Rukh (who I had heard was dropping by to wish the team good luck) and . . . of course, finally . . . being directed by Yash ji!

Sometimes, good stress really helps, with that tinge of nervous energy.

I had heard my directors call out 'Action' before too, but that day was different. That day, Yash ji was saying 'Action' to me and I was HIS actor. My daydreams merged with reality that moment . . . Dreams do come true.

The magic of that 'Action' was such that I performed without a single glitch. All actions were performed as told, all lines of the long monologue were in place and, the exuberant Shabbo had found her *sur* (tone)!

I don't know if it was for me but the first shot of *Veer-Zaara* got a round of applause and I happened to be a part of that shot. I was truly overwhelmed and went up to Yash ji.

'Yash ji.'

He turned around. '*Bahut ache, beta* (Very good, child).' He patted my back and left to set up the next shot.

I stood there even after he had left and I could absolutely relate to that feeling when you are so happy that you begin to cry. I was absorbing and cherishing each moment of being directed by him. Every once in a while, I'd remind myself, 'Hey you! Guess who is directing you?' And then, I'd feel on top of the world and absolutely fortunate!

As the shoot progressed, the formal conversation with
Yash ji gave way to fun Punjabi banter and I became his dessert
companion on the sets. Whenever meetha (sweets) used to
be served (and there were quite a few delicacies on Yash Raj
sets), Yash ji used to send for me and we'd have them together,
discussing them at length—the love for sweets of the two
Punjabis was very evident.

I had warmed up to Yash ji as a person too and really enjoyed
talking to him. So much so that after we finished shooting, I'd
go to the Yash Raj office and chat with him. He had become
that someone who I shared a lot with and sought all advice
from, and he too gave it to me with a sense of belongingness.
He was so full of warmth despite his stature. That's when I
started calling him Yash uncle. From being an ardent admirer
to calling him that had been a journey in itself and I was myself
mesmerized by it.

Soon, the film was ready for release. The premiere was
organized on a grand scale at the huge Inox Theatre, where
the who's who had been invited. It was a big day for me. How
would the audience react to my role? Would I be the next 'best
friend' in business? These questions kept crossing my mind but
I trusted Yash ji and Aditya to have presented me beautifully.

With a mixed bag of thoughts and holding Ma's hand, I
entered the premiere and went straight to Yash ji. He greeted
me warmly and said, 'Hello beta, all set?'

I smiled and then went inside the auditorium with Ma.

The film started and I was wonderstruck by what I was
watching. Yes, the grandeur, love, friendships, the awesome
storytelling . . . everything that I loved in a Yash Chopra film
was there. The only add-on was that now, I was a part of it too!

A surge of pride seeped in, at just belonging to a film
like that, in whatever capacity. With that thought, Ma and I

happily went out during the interval to get snacks. Suddenly, I was surrounded by the crowd, by the industry folks! 'OMG! Are you the one playing Shabbo in the film?' they asked. I was overwhelmed! I hadn't seen this kind of adulation before!

I ran to Yash ji. He was already surrounded by a crowd but he saw me and reached out. *'Pata hai, sab mujhe pooch rahe hain Shabbo kaun hai?* Is she a new girl? Did you get her from Pakistan?' He was smiling as he said that.

A renowned actor came up to him, 'Sir, absolutely loving the film! Beautiful love story. Who's that girl who plays Shabbo, sir?'

Yash ji pulled my hand and brought me forward, 'She. Her name is Divya Dutta.'

I was elated to see everyone coming out saying, 'Who's that girl?'

I could only look up and thank the universe. In the most unassuming way, I had actually been launched by Yash Chopra—my introduction to the world of commercial cinema. And yes, I had arrived! In a true Yash Chopra way!

I could never thank Yash ji and Aditya enough for keeping their word. 'You will always be remembered for *Veer-Zaara*,' they had said. Yes, I am.

After *Veer-Zaara*, my chats with Yash ji continued. It gave me a lot of peace to go and spend an hour, and just talk to him. I used to come back happy and somewhere, I also felt privileged.

Yash ji had a very good habit. He would always call everyone he was close to on their birthday. It would be a one-liner but it meant a lot. *'Haan ji, beta.* Happy birthday, take care.' He would hang up and I would still be beaming.

The last time I met him was at the premiere of his next film, *Jab Tak Hai Jaan*. A special set had been erected for the premiere to give it a royal look, befitting the star filmmaker.

I still remember my last chat with him! He and Pam aunty (his lovely wife) were leaving the theatre after the screening. I saw him and called out from behind. He turned and across the row of seats and amidst the crowds, we shook hands. 'Yash uncle, how are you?' I shouted out.

'*Bas theek! Release ho jaye film to uske baad free,*' he smiled.

In a few days, I heard the news of his passing. It was too shocking. His smiling face and my time with him played in my head like a film. I had never seen him dull or low, ever. He was always smiling. He was always inspiring.

Even today, when I think of him, I have a broad smile. Because he left us with that—the huge legacy of films he made with so much love.

A filmmaker like him is born once in a lifetime.

I'll never get enough of watching and rewatching his films and falling in love with Hindi cinema again and again.

Thank you, Yash uncle, for the movies, for the warmth, and for being my dessert companion. Thank you for this dream journey I had with you.

The lyrics of your song from Kabhi Kabhie *reverberate, 'Wo bhi ik pal ka kissa the, main bhi ik pal ka kissa hun, kal tumse juda ho jaunga, jo aaj tumhara hissa hun . . . (They were also there for a moment, so was I. Tomorrow I will be gone, even though I'm a part of you right now).'*

You'll never cease to be a hissa (part) of our lives. You live in us through your beautiful films and here's a toast to you and your movies.

Now and always.

SONU NIGAM

I was speeding in my car to that one destination. That house that I always went to when I was down and out. I had just broken-up with the guy I was dating, and instead of heading home, I turned my car towards Sonu's house—he who shooed away all my worries with his warm, reassuring smile, and yes, not without pulling my leg. I ran up to his house and went to his room unannounced. He was getting ready for a concert and was surprised to see me, until, of course, he saw the tears in my eyes.

'Motu' is what he has endearingly called me always (whether I have lost or gained weight). So, he asked, '*Kya hua, Motu? Ro kyu rahi hai?* (What happened, Motu? Why are you crying?)'

He hadn't even completed the sentence and I burst out crying. I guess it happens when you are with someone whom you feel most comfortable with and can let down your guard. It's the most beautiful feeling to be just yourself with someone, totally transparent. No fear of being judged, no stress of putting on a formal front, and that has been my equation with Sonu Nigam. I call him my soul friend.

He made a quick call to his manager that he would leave in half-an-hour, and save time by getting ready at home. He wanted to hear me out. '*Accha* Motu, I have a concert. Do you mind if I get ready while you talk?' I nodded even as I continued crying. He went to his dressing room to start putting on make-up, and I followed him like a little lamb and sat on the stone shelf under the mirror so I could face him while blurting out my woes.

He offered me a glass of water and then I started telling him about the bitter fight I had had with my boyfriend, and how I had called it quits, and this and that, and well, that was that. There was nothing more to say. The tears had automatically stopped too. I had vented. I was feeling lighter, a huge change from how I was feeling when I had entered. But the handsome man in front of me looked the same—calm—until he smiled and then laughed at my naivety and made light of my situation by imitating me. And I didn't realize when I started laughing— at myself and at what had happened to me just a few hours ago. He changed my perspective on the situation. I could either cry about it or laugh about it and move on. The latter is what he always taught me, without really making an effort to teach. His presence was enough, a very precious one at that.

I had met him when I had just begun my career—he was already a heart-throb, a rage. His then girlfriend and now wife, Madhurima, had become a friend of mine on the sets of a very popular show, *Superhit Muqabla*, which I was hosting at that time (Sonu had hosted it super successfully before me). One day, she visited me at home, and we chatted nineteen to the dozen. And she mentioned that her boyfriend was coming to pick her up. When I came out to drop her, I saw a swanky red car waiting for her, and just like a scene from a Hindi film, someone got out in style. What an entry, I thought as I looked at his face. It was Sonu Nigam!

I held my breath. Madhu introduced us. Of course, he needed no introduction, but I was surprised that he knew me. He met me very warmly and then we chatted for a few minutes before they left. That was it, until two years later.

I got a call from Sonu's dad, Agam ji, a prolific singer himself. He asked me if I'd be interested in hosting a Sonu Nigam show in the US. He added that the tour would be for two months. I have always had travel phobia—a fear of a change of place, away from home. Two months sounded like a long time. I called my mom, who was in Punjab at that time, and asked her if she thought I could manage two months on my own. She laughed and said, 'When you go with good people, they become family. Go. Enjoy. It will be a memorable experience.'

And what a memorable experience it was! It gave me a friend for life. We started our tour and the grandeur of it all mesmerized me. Sonu is a dream to watch on stage. The audience just couldn't get enough of him—girls going insanely crazy, the applause, the huge auditoriums, NRIs getting emotional on hearing Sonu sing, and so much more. He knew how to hold his audience, to captivate them with his sheer presence, and then the way he charmingly interacted with them, as if he knew them all personally, joking and chatting between performances. And of course, those performances—sometimes, I got so spellbound just watching him that someone backstage had to nudge me on cue to go on stage. It was all so new to me and I was trying to absorb it all. Then I would go on stage and announce the next act with the beautiful lines that my mother had written out.

It was all going well. We would perform in one city, go out, do some *masti*, see places, and then move to another city.

This went on for a month and I began to feel a bit homesick. I didn't have a mobile phone at that time. I would go out to a phone booth to call my mom and speak to her. In the city that we were in, I couldn't find a phone booth. One morning, some of the other singers and I were in the gym. Sonu just dropped in. He briefly chatted with the girls and while talking to me, he felt something was amiss.

He then asked me what was wrong. The moment he asked, my eyes welled up like a child. I said, 'I'm missing Ma.'

He smiled and then laughed and took out his mobile. '*Number bol aunty ka* (Give me your mother's number).' I can't explain the joy and gratitude I felt at that moment. He saw me chat with Ma from a distance. He saw me smiling again, and when I went to return the mobile, he just said, '*Rona nahi Motu, main hun na. Jab baat karni ho le lena phone* (Don't cry Motu, I'm here. Whenever you need to talk, take my phone).'

I never cried on that trip again; well, not for the same reason at least. In yet another city, we were all backstage. It was tradition for the entire group to shut their eyes, hold hands, and pray before every show. It was an exceptionally large auditorium. I was a bit nervous, though I was ready with my lines.

Unfortunately, before the concert started, the ACs in the auditorium conked out. Gradually, we could feel the audience getting restless. It was getting warm and stuffy, but as they say, the show had to go on. So, we continued. It was my turn to go recite some poetic lines and then announce another singer. As I went on stage, some boys sitting in the front row started hooting and passing remarks. Their edginess due to the heat was affecting me. I kept looking straight, trying to ignore what they were saying, and continued with my lines.

But the remarks got loud and the hooting even louder, to the point where I couldn't take it any more and ran backstage. Yes, in tears. Predictably, the knight in shining armour came to my rescue, but in the bargain, he taught me a lesson for life as an artist. The singer I had announced had started singing. In the meanwhile, everyone had told Sonu what had happened, and he came looking for me (I was sitting upset in a corner).

He held my hand and pulled me up on stage. I didn't understand what he was up to. He stopped the performance, and told the audience that he wanted to have a word. I had heard that Sonu was very straightforward and always spoke his mind. That day, I saw it for the first time.

He was angry, actually, he was hurt. He took the mic and addressed the bunch of boys. 'Is it our fault that the ACs conked out? In spite of it, we are performing for you, dancing and singing with full energy, not bothering about how hot it is, because we are here to entertain fellow Indians who are away from their homeland, and we are here to bring you the warmth of your country. And what do we take back as memories? That you hooted at a girl who's come from your country to entertain you?'

There was pin-drop silence. No one spoke. The boys in the front row sat with their heads down in absolute shame. Sonu broke the silence again. 'Do you want us to perform or should we go?' Everyone cheered. I could hear loud apologies, I could hear 'sorry' from different corners of the auditorium. 'Sonu ji, please perform. We are sorry!'

And then, I saw the calm Sonu again. The one with that bright charming smile. He continued to speak. 'Then cheer up this girl who should go back with good memories of you.' The audience in the huge three-storeyed auditorium shouted my name! The boys in the front seat got up first to give me a standing ovation, and then the entire audience. I doubt I'll ever forget that. Yes, the crybaby had tears in her eyes again, but of joy this time. What felt heartwarming was the way Sonu had protectively held my hand, and while I held his hand, I spoke my lines to the cheering audience.

As we were going back, he stopped me, and strictly said, 'Don't stick to mugged lines. Mould yourself like clay in every situation. Keep changing your lines according to the kind of audience you are with. Chat with them, interact with them, make them feel like you are aiming your lines at each one of them. Don't just say the lines, feel them for who you are saying it to, that matters a lot.' I stood backstage, shaken. Too much had happened in the past hour. Here was a guy who stood by me, fought for me, and then scolded me for my betterment like someone who felt responsible for me.

For my next announcement, I left my script behind. No more mugged up lines alone!

I went and cracked a joke, then picked someone from the audience to chat with. I could feel that my equation with the audience had changed. They were literally eating out of my hands. I was gradually gaining confidence and my smile had come back too. I just looked backstage once. Yes, he was there. Standing and looking over, watching his little friend come into her own.

Sometimes, just knowing someone is there for you can give you so much strength. That day, Sonu standing there to see me on stage instead of going to his green room to change, gave me wings and I fluttered to newer heights.

To date, I have never followed only scripted lines on stage. I always mix and match, chatting with the audience, making them my own. That's the magic and that's the mantra. I am considered one of the topmost hosts today, and I have that one friend to thank for it.

When we came back, we stayed in touch, meeting once in a while. And it was always the same with him—laughing off worries, making fun of situations and realizing, after all, that the problems weren't bigger than our willpower to overcome them.

Somehow, one aspect of my life was never hidden from Sonu—my so-called personal life. In fact, he used to joke that my relationships were disastrous for me—like I was holding a gun to my own head. One fine day, a common friend of ours was visiting from Canada and Sonu had called me to meet her. But I was going through yet another break-up, and was inconsolable. My mom picked up the phone and told him what was happening. In an hour, the doorbell rang and in came Sonu, with our friend. Both of them came straight into my room which was all dark, reflecting my mood, obviously. He switched on the light and came in with a bright, happy hello. Both of them sat with me and he said, 'You are at it again? You're holding a gun to your head again?'

I couldn't help but smile. Suddenly, Sonu asked, 'You want to feel better?' I nodded. 'Go get your boyfriend's picture.' I was a bit taken aback, but did what I was asked to. I placed it on the table. 'Now, get some darts and rotten tomatoes,' he ordered. What was he doing? I was in no mood to even see the boyfriend, well, ex-boyfriend's picture. 'Now, throw the tomatoes on the picture!'

I thought he was joking, but he meant it. He handed me a tomato and said, 'Throw it and say what's in your heart, blurt out your anger.'

In no time, I had thrown all the tomatoes and darts, used the choicest expletives and ruined the newly painted wall. But what the heck! I was laughing. They were laughing with me. Ma was laughing too, on seeing me laugh. *Bas, itni si baat thi!* (That was all!) That man in the picture for whom I had been crying buckets only a few minutes ago seemed insignificant suddenly. The past did not seem to matter. What mattered was a friend sitting right in front of me, who had a broad twinkling smile on his face on seeing me laugh. I knew it meant the world to him to see me happy.

Years passed, but Sonu and I were always in touch however busy he would be. He would always be the first one to know what was happening in my life. He constantly encouraged me; whenever we met at get-togethers, he would tell everyone, '*Ye ladki apne dum par kahan se kahan aa gayi* (This girl has reached here on her own capabilities).' I could see the genuine pride he felt while saying that.

I would drop by at his recordings just to see him at work, all passion! So effortlessly, he'd finish recording a song in no time. Sonu was also extremely close to his mother and was severely affected when he lost her to cancer. He was always strong, of course, but I could see him trying to find answers to life, death, loss and more. He had become more spiritual to find peace within. I looked forward to my once-in-a-while chat sessions with him. We'd sit, talk, laugh, and then I'd hear his amazing philosophies on life, which he had gathered from life itself, always more mature than his age. It was intriguing to hear him.

He was there in my lowest phase—when mom went—right next to me, literally a pillar of strength. He never let me fall. Whenever I am extremely happy or sad, there's one phone call I have to make, to him.

During the lockdown, I was on video call with him, laughing, joking, and then, he just said out of the blue, '*Motu, tu theek hai na? Kuch chahiye toh nahin?*' He asked me whether I was okay and if I needed anything. I was quiet for a long time. No, I wasn't thinking if I wanted something. I was trying to absorb what he had said. In many years of being on my own, I'm not used to a man asking me that, that too with such a sense of belonging and affection.

You, my dear Sonu, have the ability to bring me tears of joy. And there are very few people who you can just be yourself with, with your craziness, idiosyncrasies, weaknesses, tears, everything.

Everyone knows you for your strengths, but there are a few who know and love you for your weaknesses too.

You, Sonu, are that for me—the one who's always reminding me to laugh in tough situations, to face life head-on. You are my soul friend, who's always wiped my tears off with a smile and that hearty laughter. You are the one holding my hand always, even from a distance, from where I can always hear your magical voice in my ears, 'Motu, tu theek hai na?'

SHAH RUKH KHAN

All the girls I knew had a crush on him! We all waited with bated breath to watch him on Doordarshan. Hearts fluttered, there were deep sighs, and all the girls swooned over him—he was the rage! Abhimanyu Rai *urf* Abhi from *Fauji*.

Who would ever forget him in that?

He was the topic of discussion among all the girls in my college, with each one claiming their sole right over the teen sensation. Some of them also broke up with their boyfriends because of their new-found loyalty to this charming boy with a dimpled smile.

As for me, no matter what—exams or family or friends— when it was *Fauji* time, everyone knew Divya got transported to another world. I used to wait to get a glimpse of his dimpled smile, as if it was only reserved for me. The actress opposite him was a nice girl, but I hated her. I, like many other girls, thought his deep intense looks and smile were only for me. *Bas mere liye . . .*

One fine day, during one of the break periods in college, we were all sitting under our favourite tree sharing tiffins and gossip when a girl ran up to us, absolutely breathless. She could barely find words to tell us the news. 'Did you hear that Abhi from *Fauji* is coming to our college?' Everyone froze for a moment. That couldn't be true! Why would he?

My best friend jolted out of her reverie before any of us did and asked her the same question. 'Why would he come here?'

'Oh, you don't know? He's our senior Ritu's cousin and he's coming to pick her up. I just overheard. Lucky Ritu, man!'

The food and tiffins were left lying around as everyone rushed to the gate. Word had spread. Half the college was out, trying to hide from the prying eyes of teachers and waiting to catch a glimpse of the heart-throb! Some were pretending to read books in the garden; others were just strolling, and some were having golgappas outside. But all eyes were on the gate. Two hours passed by but there was no sign of Abhimanyu Rai! I was the class captain. So, it was my duty to get the girls inside the class but I was heading the herd instead.

Suddenly, I saw some activity around me. I saw everyone looking in the same direction, but it wasn't towards the gate. Ritu was marching towards us. There was pin-drop silence around. We were all expecting her to tell us when he was arriving. We waited for her to speak. She did. And pulled the rug from under our feet. 'You crazy girls! I was just joking. Abhi is not my cousin. I had cooked up a story in front of my group just to boast around and your silly friend overheard it and spread it like wildfire! Now go back to your classes!'

None of us moved, hoping that she was faking it. She started walking back and then paused dramatically. 'By the way, his name is Shah Rukh Khan!'

What! My Abhimanyu Rai had a different name? He was Shah Rukh Khan! I didn't know that but my feelings for that dimpled charmer remained unchanged. For years, I ardently watched all his work, daydreamed and smiled. Maybe someday I'd meet him.

And then, as destiny would have it, I joined the movies. After my initial training with *Stardust* magazine's academy, I had started doing what is probably the toughest thing to do in the film world—doing the rounds of producers' offices. I was a shy, inhibited girl. So, I didn't really know the protocol. Wherever I went, I took a bunch of my pictures along (the glamorous ones where I wouldn't recognize my own self).

One day, I had gone to the production house that was producing *Baazigar*. I was told that I was being considered too. And then I was told that the hero was Shah Rukh Khan! I met the producers and the directors, Abbas-Mustan, and they looked pretty happy about shortlisting me. As I was walking down the steps, I bumped into someone who was rushing up the stairs, and all my photographs fell out of my bag.

'Oops, sorry!' He looked at me.

I froze! It was him! Yes, it was!

As I stood dumbfounded and speechless, he picked up my scattered photographs and handed them to me.

'Hi, I am Shah Rukh! You are Divya, right? Hope to work together! Good luck!' And he walked past, with that dimpled smile.

I stood there motionless, trying to absorb what had just happened. He knew my name! And he had wished me good luck! I pinched myself. Yeah, I wasn't daydreaming! This time that dimpled smile was for me! I was blown away by his charm. He had cared to remember the name of one of the shortlisted actors! Wow! I had finally met *the* Shah Rukh Khan!

That film didn't happen for me. And off went my dream of making my debut with Shah Rukh. But opportunities do knock at your doorstep. One fine day, I got a call from a friend telling me that Mani Ratnam was looking for a parallel lead in his film, *Dil Se*. Manisha Koirala had already been signed up. I was given

Mani sir's number so that I could talk to him. I was a nervous wreck. Shy and awkward, I didn't know how to call up *the* Mani Ratnam and ask him directly to cast me! I mean, he wouldn't even have known who I was.

Then one of my friends said, 'Why don't you ask Shah Rukh to help?'

And I replied, 'But he doesn't know me well either. We'd just bumped into each other once for a few seconds!'

The friend impatiently said, 'Listen, when you really want something, you must find a way!'

I thought of all possible ways but no solution came to me. None of the biggies were my friends. In fact, I had no contacts. I had just arrived from Ludhiana, literally not knowing anyone in Bollywood. *Who would help?*

Then I realized that Shah Rukh's secretary, Anwar, was a common friend. I requested him to organize a meeting with Shah Rukh, explaining to him what I wanted to meet him for. Anwar had a warm smile on his face, more of amusement I would say. He must have been thinking, 'This little kid doesn't want to leave any stone unturned.' He agreed to organize a meeting with Shah Rukh but also said that was all he would be able to do. I thanked him immensely!

I was told that Shah Rukh was already in Delhi, shooting for *Dil Se*. Those were the early days of mobile phones and I didn't have one. I was told to stand at a spot, at a certain time, and that someone would come and escort me to meet Shah Rukh.

I dressed up in my best salwar kameez and hired a cab to reach Connaught Place, where he was shooting. But I wasn't prepared for what I saw. It seemed as if all of Delhi had landed in Connaught Place. Everyone present was shouting his name. People were jumping over one another to get a glimpse of him! *But where was he?* Suddenly, I saw the cameraman and the crew following a young man who was running and jumping over the railing. He seemed to be chasing someone . . . *That* was him! So full of energy, so full of enigma. He was obviously in the midst of a shot and the crowd was cheering for him in unison! 'Shah Rukh! Shah Rukh!' It was unbelievable! I was cheering too, somewhere within, for my favourite man.

After about half-an-hour of standing at the assigned spot, I kind of gave up hope. Why would he remember that a meeting had been fixed with this newcomer, I thought to myself. That too in all that chaos. He must be too preoccupied with that tough action sequence, I reasoned. I turned back; a tad bit sad. I was thinking I would call up Anwar and tell him that I couldn't get past the crowd. Immersed in my own thoughts, as I took a few steps, I heard someone call out, 'Excuse me? Are you Divya Dutta?' My face lit up! I nodded. 'Please come, sir is waiting for you.'

That moment was unforgettable: A full security cordon surrounded me and they were piercing their way through the flood of gathered people. Everyone was staring. 'Who is this girl getting so much attention? Is she a heroine?' I could hear the murmurs.

During those days, there were no vanity vans. I was escorted to a car. It was parked in a corner but was surrounded by people shouting Shah Rukh's name, hoping to get their favourite star to say hi!

All that was happening seemed surreal to me. I couldn't make out the difference between reality and my dream world! All these years, I had imagined that someday I would meet Shah Rukh. And here, among the lakhs of people gathered, I was being escorted to meet him. I had dreamt that the dimpled smile would flash just for me some day. The car door opened and a hand came out to help me in. There it was—the billion-dollar smile—just for me. It was him!

'Hi! Apologies that we are meeting in such chaos but this is the only free time I have. Will you have some tea?'

I didn't know whom to react to! This charming man I was finally sitting next to, or the thronging crowd that was banging and shaking the car from outside for a bit of his attention!

He folded his hands in request and asked the crowd to give him some space. Then he turned his attention towards me! 'Yes, dear girl, I was told you wanted to meet me. How may I help you?' There was so much warmth in his voice that all my nervousness and apprehensions flew out of the window. I thanked him for meeting me and then told him everything: how I had heard that there was another role opposite him and how I was sceptical about talking to Mani sir directly and if he could help put in a word . . . (that was all I could muster. The rest of my feelings and words all stayed inside).

As the car kept being shaken by the fans, someone passed a cup of chai to me! Shah Rukh gestured to me to have it. I could sense envious glances all around but Shah Rukh was unperturbed. With a bright smile, he said, 'Sure, I'll convey your message to Mani sir. Let's hope for the best!' And despite knowing fully well that the crowd would go berserk if he moved out, he chivalrously escorted me out; waved a warm goodbye and went back to his action sequence.

He didn't need to meet me, but he did. I was just another newcomer. But he was patient enough to hear me out. He was warm enough to make me feel special. He had made a newcomer feel so important that it left me with a bright smile.

From that day, in a different way, Shah Rukh Khan became very special to me . . . truly special. The Shah with a golden heart! And that day my infatuation gave way to another stronger emotion for him—respect.

A week later I got the chance to speak to Mani sir. Shah Rukh had kept his word and conveyed the message. I called up Mani sir. This time, I was slightly self-assured. I had an introduction, at least. He spoke to me very politely and said, 'I saw your pictures. They are really nice but the problem is that you bear an uncanny resemblance to Manisha Koirala and she's already the leading lady in the film. Since you are not supposed to be sisters in the film, it will technically look wrong. But I do hope we can work together soon.' I was disappointed but I also had the satisfaction of having tried my best; of having a superstar who didn't even know me well coming to offer a helping hand. And I did understand Mani sir's point of view when I finally saw the film. He was right.

However, sometimes giving something your best too is a very satisfying feeling. Whatever you do, do it dil se…

The next time I met Shah Rukh was on the sets of *Veer-Zaara*. I had already shot for the film and was waiting impatiently to shoot with him. Finally, it happened in Delhi.

My first day of a shoot with Shah Rukh! In the scene, he was bidding me goodbye while leaving for India. Kirron Kher was part of the scene too. I was excited and all set to shoot! And then, he arrived. The energy on the set changed! He met everyone and finally came up to me. 'How are you, Divya? I believe you are doing a super job!' I tried to speak but could only manage a smile and probably mumbled a 'Thank you'. Then he took me aside and said, 'Hey, tell me about the dialect you are using na . . . and how would I say, "Okay bye, I am leaving" in that dialect?' I felt so nice that he was trying to improvise so beautifully, automatically creating a bond between Shabbo (the character I played) and Veer (him, obviously)! That was the ease and effortlessness he brought to his acting!

He finally picked up, '*Main julla han*' as his final words to me in that scene.

We did a rehearsal and before the shot, Shah Rukh whispered in my ear, 'You must make sure you are not covered by the other actors.' He was pointing to the camera angle. Since I wasn't too aware of camera angles, my face was hidden by mistake but it was promptly corrected by my most amazing co-star! I took my correct position and the scene happened in one go.

Afterwards, I went up to him. This time, I did not fumble or mumble. 'Thank you, Shah Rukh! Means a lot to me.'

From that day onwards, I shared a special bond with him! Laughing and joking on the sets; improvising shots; listening to stories from the days when he started out, and his dreams and aspirations. He spoke about how, with no *filmi* background, he had made it big and the promises he had made to himself when he had first stood by the sea in Mumbai . . .

One day, we were shooting a scene where I was required to abruptly get up from the charpoy and rush to Shah Rukh. I conveniently forgot that the wall behind me was made of plaster of Paris (PoP). Every time I got up, I used to brush against it and in the process, break it a little each time! We did four to five takes for that scene. I could see that Shah Rukh had an amused smile on his face seeing my clumsiness. I went up to him and Yash uncle and apologized.

'Sorry! I'll take care this time, I promise!'

And I went back to the charpoy, telling myself not to goof up this time. As Yash uncle said 'Action', in my eagerness to please, I got up even more abruptly and the entire PoP wall fell on me. I was taken aback. The entire unit was silent and then I saw Shah Rukh. He had tears in his eyes and I saw that he was cracking up! Laughter is so infectious! I was feeling like a fool but even I couldn't control myself as our eyes met. We both broke into a crazy bout of laughter. The wall was mended quickly enough and everyone was ready to shoot again but Shah Rukh and I were still laughing. Yash uncle joked, '*Chalo, in dono ko hans lene do, hum chai pi kar aate hain* (Let these two laugh, we'll have a cup of tea and come back).'

Veer-Zaara was special and working with Shah Rukh even more so. I wish we work together again. I really do. We keep bumping into each other at social gatherings. The most memorable one was when we were all returning from the IIFA Awards in Hong Kong. The flight was chock-a-block with industry folk. Javed Akhtar, Anupam Kher, Abhishek Bachchan, Shahid Kapur, Vidya Balan, Shah Rukh, Ma and me! Shah Rukh suggested that we all play dumb charades. My mom was sitting in the first row watching *Gangs of Wasseypur*. So, whenever it was someone's turn to act out the next clue, they would have to go and stand next to her. When it was Shah Rukh's turn, he unintentionally touched her screen, not once but thrice, and hit the rewind button each time in the process. I saw that mom ended up watching the same scene thrice. However, when Shah Rukh charmingly said, 'Oops! Sorry aunty!' Ma was, obviously, all smiles. Thank god she didn't say, 'You can do it again, beta. I'll watch this scene a few more times!'

After we were all done with the game, we decided to nap for a bit. In a while, someone knocked at my seat very softly. I woke up to see Shah Rukh. 'Hey,' he said giving me a packet of goodies he'd bought on the flight. 'This one's for you!'

I was speechless. It was so very thoughtful of him. He had given one to all of us with that disarming smile. When we landed, people thronged around him. Fortunately, his security team took over and whisked him away. I had the feeling that I hadn't even got the opportunity to say bye to him. Ma and I walked out of the airport only to see him waiting for us. In spite of the crowd, he was there to make sure the ladies sat in their cars first! Only after that did he leave but not before flashing that warm dimpled smile of his.

Shah, as I love to call him, will always remain the most charming and supportive co-actor. There's enigma and energy when he's around. Yes, maybe someday I'll work with him again. Someday, I'll burst into peals of laughter with him again. Him . . . my Abhimanyu Rai. From then to now, it's been an amazing journey of knowing him. And yes, from waiting for him at the college gate to being dropped by him to my car, life had come full circle.

Dreams do come true when you wish for them, dil se. Hain na, Shah Rukh?

SHYAM BENEGAL

Mandi was etched in my memory. Since the time I saw it as a kid, I just couldn't get it out of my head—the performances, the scenes and the climax! What made it even more exciting was watching it when I had been told to stay out of the room. When I innocently went up to Ma later and asked her who had made it, she replied, 'Arey, he's a brilliant director— Shyam Benegal. I'll show you his work when you grow up a bit so that you absorb it better.'

That name stayed with me . . . Shyam Benegal. And, of course, in a few years, I had seen all his movies. I took pride in saying that he was one of my most favourite directors.

I had a bucket list of filmmakers I wanted to work with after I joined the movies. I had met some of them but somehow hadn't been able to find a way to meet Shyam Benegal.

I finally did, at the premiere of *Train to Pakistan*. After the film, a lot of people kept coming to congratulate me. I saw my friend Rajeshwari Sachdev talking to a gentleman . . . yes, it was him! I left the people around me and ran to meet him. Rajeshwari saw me rush in and introduced us, 'Hey Divya, meet Shyam babu'. Shyam babu, as he's endearingly addressed by everyone, greeted me warmly and said he had liked my work in the film. I thanked him and hesitatingly asked if I could come and meet him someday. He nodded very pleasantly and graciously gave me his number.

'Call me and come next week,' he said.

Wow! That was simple.

Before I knew it, I was sitting in his office. All the walls were covered with posters of movies I had loved watching as a kid! In about ten minutes, the peon came and said, 'Sir is calling you. *Aaiye*!'

His room was full of books and he was sitting in the corner, reading something.

'Come my dear! How are you?'

Life can be so intriguing. I had been telling the world that I would love to meet Shyam Benegal someday and now that he was sitting in front of me, words eluded me. I kept crushing the poor little tissue paper in my hand and mustered a belated, 'How are you sir? I am fine!' All in the same breath.

He smiled.

I am sure he could gauge that I was nervous. 'Have some tea,' he said and asked for two cups to be brought in.

After an awkward silence, I managed, 'Sir . . . err, Shyam babu, I would so love to work with you. Do you have something for me in your next?'

I wasn't used to asking anything from anyone but with him, I felt I could. It felt so right.

He thought for a moment and rolled up his fingers to make a lens-like gesture and looked at me through it. I'll never forget that moment! And the pause after it. I waited with bated breath as he sat thinking. 'Okay, young lady! So, I already have a cast for my film *Samar* . . .' My heart sank. He then continued, '. . . but there's a dance number in it . . . a folk number. Would you like to do it?'

I was about to stand up and jump but I controlled myself, 'Yes, of course, Shyam babu!'

'Okay, lovely. I shall ask the team to give you all the details. See you then,' he said.

I pinched myself as I walked out. In my experience in the industry till then, I was used to promises being made but never being fulfilled. And here was a man who had just met me, and instantly told me what he had to offer. No postponing. No promises. That is Shyam babu! Always honest, clear and straightforward. He says things the way they are and offers the best possible solutions for every query. Nothing complicated. He made me wonder: if everything can be that simple, why do people complicate it? And that, I think, is the sign of a genuinely successful man and achiever who is so secure with himself that he does not need to derive it by rubbing his powerful status on others. On the contrary, his simplicity surprised me. He never said, 'Call my manager', even though I was a rank newcomer. He said, 'Call me if you have any queries, lady!'

I went back humming and dancing, counting the days till I would join him at the shoot in Sagar, Madhya Pradesh (MP). I was debuting in a Shyam Benegal film with a dance number! That was special since Shyam Benegal movies mostly don't have song and dance numbers. And yes, I was finally working with *the* Shyam Benegal!

I was informed well in advance that everyone would be travelling by train and staying at the same hotel.

In those days, I had no man Friday or personal staff travelling with me, so I was alone. But, very meticulously, I had been booked with some other crew members, so I didn't face any problems.

Sagar is a very small town in MP. So, there were two hotels there for the crew. Unfortunately, my friends Rajit Kapur and .

Rajeshwari were in the other hotel along with Shyam babu and Seema Biswas. My hotel was lovely but all the people I was familiar with were in the other one, so I felt a bit alone.

Not for too long though. I was told that Shyam babu had called me to his hotel to discuss something. I was wondering what it could be. When I reached the hotel, I got a very warm welcome. Shyam babu introduced me to everyone and then later asked me, '. . . so what are your hobbies, my dear?' I excitedly said, 'Shyam babu, I love watching movies, cooking and reading.' Before I could think of more, he said, 'Okay great! So, today, this young lady will cook something for us as it's a break day!'

I had literally put my foot in my mouth! Why did I have to blurt out cooking as my hobby! New people, new place— and I had to demonstrate my cooking skills here to none other than Shyam Benegal. I obviously looked nervous. He smilingly added, '. . . and your co-actors Seema Biswas and Rajeshwari will help too! Lunch is on you, ladies! No hotel food today.'

Err. I had been called to this new hotel to cook and that too with a senior actor I had met for the first time, Seema. Thankfully, Rajeshwari was there! We decided the menu—the aloo paranthas were assigned to me, sabzi to Seema Biswas and dal to Rajeshwari.

There was an awkward silence until Rajeshwari, who had worked with Shyam babu earlier too, pointed out that he likes his actors to interact at a personal level as the chemistry translates onscreen beautifully. 'Lovely!' I thought. But how would cooking together enhance chemistry, I wondered. I got my answer soon enough. In a while, the three us were laughing, joking, helping each other out and dancing while cooking. In seemingly no time, Seema Biswas had become Seema Didi; Raj, an even closer friend, and a sumptuous meal had been prepared for the crew.

Shyam babu took the first bite of my parantha while I looked at him nervously . . . a broad smile broke out on his face. 'This is lovely, young lady, and welcome to the unit!' Through that unique welcome, Shyam Benegal had already eased me up with the unit without making me conscious. I wasn't awkward around them any more; I was laughing and joking with everyone and happily got back to the hotel I was staying in. This time, I did not feel alone.

I had been called there for a week but I was wondering why a song sequence would take a week to shoot and what could I possibly do in my free time. Yet again, there was a surprise waiting for me.

Shyam babu called for me. I had mentally prepared myself to be introduced to the choreographer and start rehearsing. I reached the set and waited for Shyam babu to finish a shot. Then he came and sat with me. 'Listen, my team is taking you to a local banjara area today. You have to spend time with them, and observe their movements and their dancing, etc. Okay? Good luck.'

Err. I didn't understand. Where was the choreographer? The warming up to the unit bit I had understood, but what was this about befriending the local banjaras? I wondered what Shyam babu had up his sleeve.

But by then, I was also getting used to these surprise elements that he liked to throw in. I reached the local *basti* and met the attractive but shy women from the community. After a bit of a formal chat, the production team told the women that I would be with them for a few hours and requested that they teach me their folk dance. They were smiling. I wasn't.

Yet again, Shyam babu had proven me wrong. He had not sent me there for the heck of it. There was a good reason for it. By the end of the day, I was yapping away with the girls, feeling one among them and dancing with them. In the process, I had mastered their dance moves. I came back happy and ecstatic! I was loving Shyam babu's way of subtly putting me in the mood for the film.

After two days, Shyam babu bumped into me at the dinner table. 'I believe you learnt well!' I smiled and he continued, '. . . so tomorrow, you will be given the song. Since you know the steps and mannerisms of the local dancers, choreograph the song your way!' I dropped the morsel in my hand. This one I surely wasn't prepared for! But I did muster enough courage to say, 'But Shyam babu, the choreographer will do that, na?'

He didn't have a smile on his face this time. Just a matter-of-fact expression. 'No. You will choreograph. Good night.' And then he was gone.

Over the next two days, I had to put all my attention into something I was doing for the first time, that too for a feature film and for none other than Shyam Benegal! I was shocked at how he had entrusted this huge responsibility on a kid with no experience! What if I goofed up? What if it wasn't what he wanted?

There was too much pressure but nervous energy does that to you and it was done sooner than I'd thought. The night after, I met him again when the unit was having dinner and mumbled, 'I choreographed the song, Shyam babu!' And I waited for him to respond. He looked up with a warm smile and said, 'Good, young lady. Now tomorrow, a hall has been booked for you in the hotel; we shall send ten dancers—please teach them what you choreographed. And yes . . . we shoot with you day after!'

I couldn't sleep! What was he up to? First learn the folk dance, then based on the steps, choreograph the song. And if that wasn't enough, teach the dancers as well and that too in a single day! How was this going to happen?

Anyway, I gave all the dancers a 7 a.m. call time because I knew I just didn't have enough time. There was too much on my plate! We rehearsed for sixteen hours straight. I was tense but also enjoying this new experience of being the choreographer. When we did our final rehearsal, I felt a sense of pride and confidence in having done it all on my own!

I told the dancers to rest the next day as we would be shooting in the night. We would just rehearse before getting ready.

As I reached the set, Shyam babu surprised me again. Not only had the entire village—where we were shooting—turned up for the shoot but the entire cast and crew of the film were there too! They were not shooting that day but had come to cheer me! That, I realized, was the beauty of being on a Shyam Benegal set. Everyone was like family, lending that much-needed support.

I thought that even if we forgot the steps, Shyam babu would break the shots, so we could retake if something went wrong. That's how I tried to reassure myself.

Then came the biggest surprise. On the set, I saw six cameras placed at different angles. And he said, 'We will treat this performance as a stage act. Only once. No retakes since you are being covered from all angles.'

My heart was in my mouth. In *one go? With the entire cast there?* I was nervous. But I was the choreographer too, so I had a responsibility towards my dancers. I went up to them and offered them some pep talk (even though I was probably the one who needed it the most at that moment). 'Okay girls, we do it only once and we make magic! If you forget, don't stop. It will come back to you, okay?' And I heard a loud cheer from the girls, 'Yes, Ma'am!' And the cheer grew. This time it was from the cast and then the villagers joined in. With that loud cheer, my nervousness turned into confidence and I promised myself to try my best to deserve that cheer from all around! I looked at that one man who had just risked so much by entrusting a little girl with the biggest sequence of the film. Yes, he was smiling, unperturbed. And calmly called out, 'Action!'

The music played; cameras rolled and I started dancing. I was in a different state of mind. I wanted to prove that it was a good decision he had taken by trusting me. I wanted to thank him too for believing in me. For trusting that I could deliver. I had to give this dance my all. I had to push myself to excel. I was thinking a trillion thoughts when I heard the distant sound of Shyam babu's 'Cut.'

Had I goofed up? Had I forgotten the steps? Were the girls okay?

I hadn't finished thinking yet and I felt as if I was being hitched up on someone's shoulder. The cast members had lifted me up in sheer delight! There was applause all around. The music was playing again, but this time everyone was dancing to celebrate a good performance. My eyes were looking for that one man. Where was he? I saw him discussing the next day's shoot with the chief AD.

I ran up to Shyam Babu and hugged him tight. I had tears of joy. 'Sir?' I asked.

'You were very good, my dear!' And he patted my back and left.

He was so chilled out about giving me this huge responsibility, surprising me every day, bit by bit. Without my realizing it, he had made me learn so many things and got me to deliver them exactly the way he wanted.

He is truly a visionary. He knew he wanted the rawness of the local dancers. He wanted a fresh approach to choreography and he trusted his actor too. With his belief in me, there was no other way but to prove him right.

I was smiling. I was crying. I was hugging my unit people. I was patting the backs of my dancers.

I was ecstatic!

In those six days, I was a changed person. The hesitation with which I had arrived had disappeared. I knew one thing that day—I could experiment; I could try things beyond my comfort zone, I could falter and get up again, and yes, I could deliver. I was dependable and I had just one man to thank for it. The one who had subtly but surely taught me how to enjoy being an actor not just in front of the camera but off it too. Absorbing the process of making a film, each and every moment.

I was to leave on the seventh day. And I went up to Shyam babu to bid him goodbye. I had developed a beautiful bond with him—the ever-smiling man with an ocean of knowledge. I choked but managed to say, 'This was the best experience for me, Shyam babu. Thank you for everything.' And just like in Hindi movies, where one takes a pause and turns dramatically, I did too.

'Can I be in all your movies if I fit in?' He smiled but didn't say anything.

You don't need to say it when you are clear within, I guess. I have been in all his movies since then. *Welcome to Sajjanpur, Netaji Subhash Chandra Bose, Samvidhaan* and a docu-feature that he made on the history of Punjab's freedom movement.

Wasn't I lucky? But I did make sure to go to meet him in his office on those non-shoot days too. Not to discuss work but just to chat with him. Shyam babu is the most knowledgeable man I know. You can talk to him on any topic. He can explain it to you in such an interesting story format that you just want to keep listening to him. He can be as conversational with someone on the set on an everyday topic as he can be with scholars discussing history, geography, politics, people, food, movies—just about anything.

I had really started enjoying his company and my one cup of chai in his office while discussing my favourite topics. Somewhere through the conversation, he would tell me in a matter-of-fact manner to keep specific dates free for his next. It was tough to keep calm whenever I heard that. Every single time. I just felt like dancing, when I got to know I'd be working with him again.

I danced the most on his shoots. The entire cast would gather post pack-up, and sing and dance together. How many units can boast of doing that in these times when the norm is to just spend time on set during shooting and going off to the vanity vans later?

Shyam Benegal's shoots are different. They are as much fun off set as they are while shooting.

I have observed that Shyam babu doesn't let his actors overprepare. Just the right dose of knowing your character and then improvising during the shot.

During *Welcome to Sajjanpur*, we had to use a different dialect. I was the last to join the cast. Everyone had become acquainted with the language but I was still getting used to it. The assistant came to me saying they were ready for the shot. I wasn't and I ran up to Shyam babu. 'Please, can I take five minutes?'

Within two minutes, I was called for the shot. I had a hundred thoughts again—the lines, the dialect, the body language and most importantly, the comfort of being in character. But I was so busy just trying to master the lines that I was a tad nervous too.

Shyam babu saw that but still went ahead coolly. I think he knows how important nervous energy is for an actor. Like teaching a child the basics and throwing them into a pool to find their own style and strokes. My subconscious mind was busy recollecting the lines; the conscious mind was present on the set, alert and ready to improvise and as Shyam babu would like it, but not say it, excel.

I recalled his mantra: If you are overprepared, you are so sure of what you want to do and don't tend to explore more possibilities during the shot whereas this little nervous energy keeps you open to experiment with newer things.

Welcome to Sajjanpur got me many awards for my role and, as it happened on most Shyam babu sets, I made many friends for life too!

Once, Shyam babu was narrating anecdotes from *Mandi* (*Mandi!* My favourite film). I was dying to find out everything about the set stories from the man himself. He was telling us how the entire cast would play *antakshari* on the bus on the way back from the shoot; how they cooked together on Shabana Azmi ji's birthday on the outdoor set and how that tough terrain they shot on became so much fun! Intrigued, I asked him, 'Shyam babu, if I was an actor at that time, which role would you have cast me in?'

I don't know why but I really wanted to know. But he just smiled and kept me guessing.

There is one incident that I'll never forget. It was when I last shot with him during the making of that Punjabi docu-feature. I was to play the anchor, reciting the story in Punjabi in verse. I wasn't worried as the assistant had told me that there would be a teleprompter and all I had to do was read.

This is going to be easy, I thought, and chirpily reached the set in my Punjabi attire. I just read the lines once to get acquainted with them. Shyam babu arrived, and as usual, patted my back and asked, 'All set, young lady?'

For a change, I was!

Then, as I started reading from the teleprompter, he shouted, 'Cut'. 'I am not liking the way you are reading. It will be more natural if you just say the lines without reading them.'

I felt the ground slipping from under my feet. 'But Shyam babu, I don't know the lines and these are a good twenty-five pages of verse!'

'No problem. I'll give you an hour. Learn.'

And he coolly went away, leaving me sweating in that Punjabi attire! I called up Ma and broke down! 'How will I learn twenty-five pages of verses in Punjabi, Ma?'

'Beta, if he's told you that, then there must be a reason, na? He probably believes that you can do it, that's why he asked you. Otherwise, why will he waste his unit's time?'

That brightened me up a bit. He did have that faith in me but I was still terribly nervous. I didn't want to let him down at all! I went behind a huge rock where we were shooting and hid myself from the world, focusing all my concentration on those twenty-five pages.

Mugging up verse is tough because if you miss one word here and there, the rhyme goes for a toss. As expected, after exactly one hour, I saw Shyam babu sitting on the set with his trademark cap. I was trembling inside, wishing that even if the assistant had hinted at something like this, I would have come prepared.

Shyam babu and his surprises!

I heard 'Action' and started off like a parrot.

When you have a point to prove, you give it your all, and when you want to keep someone's faith in you intact, then you have no choice but to deliver. And when under pressure of the positive kind, you perform better—I learnt it that day. Yet again. From the same man.

I found something in me I never knew—I had a knack for delivering better under pressure. I had wrapped the entire thing in four hours instead of taking the entire shift! Guess the man with the vision knew it. He knew what he could get out of me. He had deliberately called me unprepared, and let me put all my concentration and focus in weaving magic on the set.

I believe that he truly is a maverick who makes you meet your own self in a new way every time you work with him.

Shyam babu is an integral part of my life now. After Ma, he and his lovely wife Nira Benegal made sure they were in touch with me, asking after my well-being every few days.

It is intriguing how life unfolds. In this big city of Mumbai—the city of dreams as they call it—you come from a smaller town having grown up watching films made by a prolific filmmaker, and admiring that person. And then life throws opportunities at you—to work with him, to get to know him, learn from him and through him, discover a new actor within yourself every time. But above all, him and his better half become those people who are always there for you.

Yes, one question remains unanswered though, and as Ma would have said, surely for a reason.

Which role would he have cast me for in *Mandi*?

Some questions are more intriguing when you don't find their answers. But I'll continue to ask. Maybe, when I am on the next set with him or during our next chai session. Till then, as always, he keeps me guessing.

JUHI CHAWLA

She has been known as the sweetest girl next door on the big screen—with a million-dollar smile, tight curls and that chirpy voice. She just lights up the screen, exuding her inherent goodness and warmth.

Juhi Chawla, apart from being a huge star, has this very likeable, amiable quality about her which makes you feel she is someone you knew before.

That is also how I felt when I first met her at the shoot of Gurdas Maan's Punjabi film, *Des Hoyaa Pardes*. For me, she was the adorable heroine of *Qayamat Se Qayamat Tak;* the star from *Darr* and many others. My connect with her was only through her movies, and I had always admired her grace. Now, I was going to meet her in person for the first time.

Mrs Manjeet Maan, the producer of the film, had told me that Juhi was lovely to talk to. Mrs Maan also told me that since they were shooting in a very limited space in a narrow lane in the village for the first few days, only one vanity van could be accommodated. So, Maan saab had sweetly offered to adjust in one of the local houses we were shooting in, but Juhi and I would have to share the same van. Interestingly, that van didn't have separate coupes, just half a wall that divided the space. So, we would practically be together.

I was a bit apprehensive about Juhi agreeing to that as we were actually strangers to one another, but I was pleasantly surprised to hear that she was the one who had suggested and offered to share her space with me. She was surely different. Refreshingly different.

Soon, I was knocking at the door of the vanity van with my bag and baggage. Juhi's man Friday opened the door and I entered awkwardly. Mrs Maan, knowing that I would be hesitant, quickly followed me to get the two of us acquainted. As we entered, Juhi said a bright hello to the two of us while doing her make-up. Manjeet ji introduced me to Juhi.

'Of course, I know her! And now we are roommates,' she joked. It lightened up the atmosphere.

I managed a smile.

I was instantly thrown into close proximity with a star, and I had to be on my best behaviour so as to not annoy her in any way, I thought. I was shown the other side of the vanity van to set up my stuff. My boy came (as nervously as his actor), to put the stuff away with utmost care so as to not disturb or intrude into Juhi's space. I had strictly instructed him to be on guard and put his best foot forward. He seemed very pressured but he obviously wasn't given a choice. So, when he left the vanity, he literally tiptoed out, much to Juhi's amusement.

As everyone gradually left the van, I felt a surge of awkwardness. The chatterbox in me had been silenced. Treading softly and carefully, making minimal noise, I went to get myself a book to read. The silence was broken by her chirpy voice from the other side, 'Will you have jaggery tea? I'm ordering some.'

'Yes,' I barely managed to reply. She laughed from the other side. 'Breathe, you still have a few more days with me here.' I was truly embarrassed that she had understood what I was feeling without even looking at me across the little divider. When the jaggery tea was brought in, I heard her again, 'Come here, have tea with me.' And I quietly went and sat with her.

As we sipped our chai, she tried breaking the ice and asked about my Punjab connection. 'So, it will be super easy for you to speak both the languages as you are from here.' She was talking about the film being bilingual, with a mix of Hindi and Punjabi. I started telling her about my background and then, I gradually warmed up to her without realizing it. I went on to animatedly tell her about how I got into movies; how many of her movies I had seen, and loved. I was unstoppable.

She had very intelligently pushed the right buttons to get the fairly-new girl comfortable. The chai was over but not my chatter. I absolutely adored her—she was fun, simple, so down-to-earth, and extremely witty!

We were now on a roll!

We would finish our shots and run to the van; watch a nice film, order the best of *garma-garam* Punjabi khaana, lassi or jaggery tea. Mrs Maan would join us for chai but the unit knew that the girls were on a fun spree and the camaraderie reflected on screen. Our scenes together were super fun and spontaneous; our chemistry as sisters-in-law was enviable—we would crack a joke in between shots, and laugh and giggle.

I had gradually found a friend in Juhi. I started sharing a lot with her too, and she would quietly listen with a smile. She had seen a lot of life too, and knew it inside out. After a bit of silence, she would softly offer a very sensible piece of advice. I felt fortunate that I had her to guide me when I needed it.

After a few days, I was told my vanity van had arrived and I could shift out. Like a tenant with a heavy heart, absolutely attached to the rented house and the owner, I sadly did the needful. But our chat sessions and movie sessions continued, and so did the friendship.

We soon got back together in Manjeet Maan's next film with Gurdas Maan, *Waris Shah: Ishq Daa Waaris*. In this one we were to play friends-turned-rivals. This time we had separate vanity vans but like the previous time, we enjoyed working together. She would guide me about my costumes, make-up, and it was a delight to do a song and dance number with her. She was quick to pick up her steps and perform like a pro. I would go to my vanity and rehearse a few times to look at ease, just like her. I was inspired and amazed.

I always saw her on set with a sweet smile. Even if she had a point to make, it was always put across warmly, with a smile, and never as criticism or complaint. And I must say that was much more impactful. I started practising that too. Instead of being reactive or hyper in a given situation, I tried the Juhi mantra—as I call it—and it bore amazing results. The person it was addressed to felt more responsible to make up for what they hadn't done right. Because they were being told about it warmly, and with respect, they gave that respect back by more than making up for it. A big lesson of life learnt from this lovely one, whose depth I could always sense from the smile on her face.

When we shot for another Gurdas Maan film, *Sukhmani*, in Kashmir, she and I would go to the shikara post pack-up, and hide our faces like little girls, and have a picnic in the middle of the Dal Lake, amid a lot of jokes and masti, and hot kahwa in hand.

A few years later, we got the opportunity of working together yet again in a film called *Chalk and Duster*, which also starred Shabana Azmi. Both of them played the ideal teachers and I was the antagonist. We both enjoyed our many face-off scenes in it as rivals, and then later, sat and chatted happily.

I remember Juhi always propagating natural therapies. If any of us had a sore throat, her famous concoctions were very effective. When, during the shoot of the film, Ma had a heart issue, she advised a nature farm or retreat first—to heal the body the natural way. After all, she too had suffered for many months when her brother Sanjiv had been hospitalized.

She was among the first ones to be by my side when Ma left. Juhi had gone through the pain of losing her mom in an accident while shooting abroad. As she held my hand, I could feel that she was sharing the sentiment of a daughter having lost a parent with me. We sat in silence for very long, while she held my hand tight. Her mere presence gave me a lot of strength.

A few months later, when I was ready with my book on Ma, and Mr Bachchan had agreed to launch it, I had to think about someone to read an excerpt from the book on the occasion. I thought of Juhi. She was the perfect choice. With her warmth, sensitivity, and that smile, all of which came from the experience of having seen life and having understood it too. I called her and she instantly agreed.

To be there for someone is a quality she most definitely has, as she's always been there for me, checking on me every now and then. It's been a while since I have met her, but I know she's always a phone call away—a senior who's always been there, guiding me when I need it.

And I wonder why they say actresses can't be friends. Here's a lovely human being I call a friend for life. With that infectious warm smile and with her 'Juhi mantra' by my side, I have learnt a lot from her.

Here's to a lot of laughter, jaggery tea, and watching a lot of movies and working together in some more too. Until then, keep smiling, dear Juhi, the sweetest of them all!

RAKEYSH OMPRAKASH MEHRA

I met him for the first time when I got a call to shoot for a Samsung ad with the Indian cricket team. I was extremely excited and was told that the director was the renowned ad-filmmaker, who had also made the film *Aks*. I met Rakeysh Omprakash Mehra on the set of that ad. Tall, with long hair and a beard, he could easily have been in front of the camera too. Assuming that he would be an elusive sort of person, I said hi with some scepticism. I was truly surprised at his reaction. 'Hi, *kaisi hain aap? Bahut badhiya kaam kiya aapne* Shaheed-e-Mohabbat *mei* (How are you? You have done a fantastic job in *Shaheed-e-Mohabbat*). It's an honour to shoot with you.' I didn't know how to react. He was the complete opposite of my perception of him—warm, friendly, a bit reserved, but a man of the soil, and very humble.

I was to play a Punjabi *kudi* (girl) in the ad with the cricketers; an absolute fun ad. So, all of them, including Rahul Dravid, Suresh Raina and Harbhajan Singh, were on one side of the vanity van, and I was in the coupe next to them with a door connecting both, in case one wanted to go from one side to the other. Then Rakeysh Mehra came to my coupe and chatted for a bit, to warm me up to the environment, I guess. He explained what we'd be doing and added that the boys were looking forward to meeting me.

And then, he suggested we go meet the boys. We both knocked at their door. The reaction was instantaneous! The chatter inside suddenly reduced and then it stopped. After a few seconds, the door opened. Rakeysh took me inside, 'So, this is Divya Dutta, and she's the girl with you in the ad.' Silence ensued, followed by scattered greetings from various directions, and then they all froze. None of us knew what to talk about next. The awkwardness was apparent. Rakeysh ji felt it too and said, '*Accha* Divya, you get ready,' and sent me off. I too was relieved to get away from that strange awkwardness.

In about ten minutes, there was a loud banging on the common door. It most definitely couldn't have been the boys after the cold response I got, so who could it be? The banging continued until I sceptically opened the door. And they all poured in like a flood. But the vibe had completely changed— they were vibrant, full of life and extremely warm. Harbhajan was the first to speak. '*O tusi Gurdas Maan ji naal* Shaheed-e-Mohabbat *kiti? Pata hi nahi si. Oh, tusi te apni hi kudi ho* (You worked in *Shaheed-e-Mohabbat* with Gurdas Maan ji? I did not know that. You are one of us!)' He told the rest and they all sat and chatted with me like long-lost friends. And then Bhajji mentioned, '*Rakeysh sir ne dassya* (Rakeysh sir told us).'

I was truly amazed. So that was the magic of Rakeysh Mehra that I kept experiencing in my films with him later too, where he completely changed the outlook of people in just a few minutes of chatting with them. For me, it still remains a mystery as to what is it that he says to change people's attitudes like that. The ad went on to become extremely popular, and the chemistry between the boys and me was very evident, thanks to Rakeysh Mehra.

After this, I heard from him for *Rang De Basanti*. I was in Mauritius when I got a call from him. '*Kaisi hain aap?*' he asked warmly and then quickly added, 'So, listen, we are shooting the title song of *Rang De Basanti* with Daler Mehndi. It would be lovely to have you make an appearance in the song.'

'I would have loved to,' I responded. 'But I am shooting in Mauritius, sir.' I couldn't do it, but I was smiling. He was so keen to have me in the song and that felt so good.

A few years passed, and *Veer-Zaara* released. I was flooded with similar roles. If they were Punjabi, vivacious, chirpy roles, I was the first choice. But the rebel in me refused them all. I didn't want to go on the sets feeling and looking the same. I didn't want to be trapped in an image. So, I said no to the biggest banners, to all the huge amounts being offered to the new chirpy Punjaban in town. My mother thought I had lost the plot. She wasn't wrong—who in her right mind would say no to so much good work?

But I sat home for a year. And one day, I heard from Rakeysh ji again. By then, I was totally frustrated with what was coming my way. So, when he said, '*Hi, kaise ho aap? Mil sakte hain?* I have a role for you in *Delhi-6*.' Before he could continue, I blurted out, pre-empting what he would say, 'Sir, is it a Punjabi role?' He replied patiently, 'No, it isn't.' But I continued, 'So then it must be a chirpy, vivacious one?' He was calm. 'No, it isn't.'

Now, I was taken by surprise. By then, I had been conditioned to the fact that the industry offers you tried and tested stuff—what's proven to be successful at the box office, people tend to follow that and offer you the same. So, I asked him, a bit confused, 'Then why did you think of me?' There was a pause, and then he calmly said, 'Because I think you are an exceptional actor, and you can play Jalebi very well. Come see me at the office.'

He was different, very different. He was least bothered about the tags given to me, about the successful image of a vivacious girl being handed over to me without my consent. I wanted to shout out to the world, 'Hey, I can do other roles equally well, only if you care to perceive me differently!' But all I got was the same. He, on the other hand, seemed unaffected. He knew what he wanted. He was clear that I would play the untouchable sweeper who all the locals eyed. He saw me for what I was capable of, not what he had seen of me in my previous films. And that, to me, meant the world. When someone believes in your capabilities, unaffected by what the world at large thinks, it is nothing short of being special.

So, the next day, I sat in his office with a mug of coffee in my hand. He looked at me calmly (of course, he could see the storm of frustration in me but he didn't mention anything). There is something about him that makes you feel so at ease and heard. How many people have the knack for listening? All of us are in too much of a hurry to talk without listening to what others have to say. It's an art and Rakeysh Mehra aces it. Feeling the comfort of being heard, I blurted out all my frustration. There was no response from the other side. Just silence.

He ran his fingers through his long hair, as if thinking, and then he started narrating the role. His action was louder than a thousand words. In response to my outburst, he had offered me a role, diverse from anything I had ever done. As an actor who believed in herself, that validation was something I needed the most at that moment—the faith that there was more to me than just the image I had been given. And he had calmly given me a brilliant role, believing in his vision and his actor completely.

My workshops, to play the firebrand Haryanvi Jalebi, began. Right from the fully tattooed look, to my body language and the dialect, all preparations were in full swing. What the conservative me couldn't get comfortable with were the abusive words that I had to blurt out. He coolly came to my rescue, and told me all about Jalebi's background, how she was a fighter who had no choice but to look after herself and for that, she had to sometimes speak in the manner that men in the locality spoke to her in. I don't know how he had said it, but after that, Jalebi became a part of me. I shed all inhibitions. I was her—bold, inherently sensual (I hadn't played a sexy avatar until then), vulnerable and blunt. Except for the vulnerable part, Jalebi was the complete opposite of me.

We went to shoot *Delhi-6* in Sambhar, a place near Jaipur. A huge resort was booked for the entire team and everyone had separate bungalow-like cottages to live in. But everyone had to gather together at a common area for food. I didn't have to shoot for the first two to three days. So, when I met Rakeysh Mehra, I asked, 'Sir, all of you will go for shoots, what will I do in this huge resort all by myself?'

I felt the palpable silence again as we walked. He always took his time to absorb and process what was being said, and then come up with the subtlest and most impactful of replies. He pointed to a squirrel running past us. 'Did you see it?'

I said excitedly, 'Of course, I just adore squirrels. *Bombay mein kahan mauka milta hai* (One does not get the opportunity in Bombay).'

He added quietly, '*Exactly, ab mauka mila hai to do–teen din enjoy karo* (Now that you are getting time, enjoy these two– three days). Watch them, play with them. You won't find this leisure back home.'

He left me speechless. He was right.

Over the next two days, I sat in the garden, soaking in the winter sun, munching on nuts, throwing a few to the squirrels around, listening to music, and dozing off. I hadn't been this relaxed in a very long time. I had made friends with nature.

The film had all the legends in it—Waheeda Rehman, Amitabh Bachchan, Rishi Kapoor, Om Puri and of course, my friends, Abhishek, Sonam, Atul and Pawan too. We were a house full of people there. My shooting had finally begun and I was getting jittery. Would I be able to perform all that I had grasped? I wondered. The man in front of me was calm. I thought he'd come and give me some instructions. None.

Then I requested him to come for a second. '*Ji, farmaiye?* (Please tell me?)' he asked.

'Sir . . . ' I whispered nervously, '. . . any instructions for me?'

'*Nahi, sab badhiya* (None, all is good).' His calmness calmed my nerves, and I gave my first shot.

There were whispers on the set. Rakeysh Mehra's wife and the editor of the film, the lovely Bharathi, came up to a nervous me and said, 'Jalebi is rocking!'

I heaved a sigh of relief, but not for too long. My next scene was in front of a huge crowd, where I was to hurl abuses at the cop played by Vijay Raaz, who in turn comes to hit me. That was the litmus test. *Was I really that uninhibited as an actor? Was I capable of letting go of all my mental blocks and just be in the role?* It got tougher when I was told that Waheeda ji, Rishi ji, Om ji, everyone else was going to be on the set to watch the shot. '*Hey bhagwan, sab theek se ho jaye, meri naak na kate* (Oh god, let everything go off smoothly, please do not let me lose face),' I pleaded with someone up there.

And then, I saw that someone in front of me, calm and cool, running his fingers through his hair, discussing the shot with the director of photography (DoP).

I barely muttered, 'Excuse me, sir?' He came to me. 'Ji?' I managed to ask, 'Sir, *matlab*, err … any instructions?' 'You are already in it, nothing for you, *bas enjoy kariye*. Play someone else and be her for that time. Own her world, Divya,' he said, softly.

Whatever part of Divya with her apprehensions and inhibitions was within me, left at that moment. Jalebi took over as if on cue from the director. As I heard a distant 'Action,' I fluently spoke a dialect I wasn't too acquainted with. I used the bold lingo as if I owned it. My body language changed and I let Jalebi completely take over. From a distance, I heard 'Cut' and a huge applause. It's not every day that you see your seniors give you a cheer in unison. Divya was back and so was the tear in the corner of my eye.

I went up to everyone, as they praised me. Rakeysh Mehra patted my back and said, '*Ye chhupi rustom hai.* She knows it all and pretends to be nervous.' He made it sound as if it was child's play for me.

I gave him a big hug, and whispered, 'Thank you, for giving me Jalebi.'

I went on to be nominated and won all awards for *Delhi-6* that year. And well, what came with it again was the tag of being the next sensuous gal in town. I was flooded with similar roles. This time, I wasn't frustrated though. I was amused. I had, by now, understood the workings of the industry, and I said my fair share of 'no' to all the films again, only agreeing to the ones that sounded different.

While that happened, I enjoyed my meetings with Rakeysh Mehra and Bharathi, and our occasional coffees, stories, poetry, and life, and yes, the silences.

At a screening of a film called *Bol*, I bumped into Rakeysh ji again. During the interval, as we were having coffee, he said matter-of-factly, 'Something beautiful is happening, Ma'am. And you have to play an important role in it. *Office aaiye* (Come to my office).'

I went to the office, imagining everything that he could possibly offer me. But with him, one never knows. He only follows his instincts, unaffected by what the world thinks or perceives.

After a hot cuppa, he said softly, '*Mazaa ayega* (It will be fun). It will turn out beautiful. We are trying to recreate the life of Milkha Singh ji, and I want you to play his sister.'

Before he completed his statement the thought of being typecast in sisterly roles clouded my head. Then came a bigger blow. 'And do you know who plays Milkha ji? It's Farhan Akhtar.'

Noooo! I thought to myself, but without realizing it, I had actually spoken it out loud, and to my embarrassment, of course, he had heard it.

'Why? You don't like him?'

'Sir, you are asking me to play sister to someone I had a crush on,' I blurted out, unwittingly. I wanted him to know that the stakes were high.

He smiled and then laughed. 'So what? You are an actor. You rise above all these feelings when you perform. It is a beautiful role *aur aap kariye isse, mazaa ayega* (you have to do the role, it will be great).'

We both sat under a tree when he narrated the story to me. While he was narrating, it started drizzling, but he didn't move or get distracted. He was so immersed in the world of Milkha ji. I, who was about to get up, saw him unaffected and as if on cue, sat back, getting pulled into his storytelling, with raindrops falling lightly on me. I have never ever enjoyed a story narration as much!

Once he put me in Isri Kaur's role, I was fully there. But with him, there was no other way. Neither would I want it any other way. I was fortunate to have the most interesting workshops for this film. Milkha ji himself came to meet Farhan and me at Rakeysh ji's office. We just sat and heard him talk about his life, his victories, his losses, his sister—it was like going into a trance, listening to a highly inspirational life like that. By then, I was so excited that I couldn't wait to be on set.

I realized very late that I actually didn't have lines. I just didn't feel the lack of it any time because Isri Kaur's role was full of silences and tears for expressing everything—happiness, pain, loss, euphoria, everything. And that was a tough one. Being someone who voiced her thoughts always, this role was, yet again, completely opposite of my personality. But I remembered seeing my mother's patients in rural Punjab during my childhood. Whenever Ma asked them something, they would express through their eyes—tears of joy/pain and silence. That memory from the subconscious had come alive to play Isri Kaur.

On the sets of *Bhaag Milkha Bhaag*, I discovered the power of the subconscious mind on various occasions. On my first day in Ferozepur, I was called by Rakeysh ji to the set to just feel the ambience. I chatted with him for a while and then suddenly, he took me to meet someone. That someone was a turbaned man, with his back towards me. Rakeysh ji tapped his shoulder and he turned. He said, introducing me to the good-looking sardar, 'Meet your brother, Milkha Singh.'

I was zapped. Even in the wildest of my imaginations, I couldn't have thought of a transformation like that. I could barely recognize Farhan. He was immersed in his role. There was a reason why Rakeysh ji had called me to the set and introduced me to Farhan, playing Milkha Singh. It took away all my doubts and apprehensions of playing Farhan's sister, because he was Milkha and I would be Isri Kaur. And that was that.

I went to the guest house totally amazed. Rakeysh ji has the knack for making you realize things without making any noise about it. One wouldn't even get to know and yet, there would be a huge transformation that he would bring about.

I will always remember a scene I was doing with the younger Milkha, played by ten-year-old Japtej. It was a very sensitive scene where he sees his sister being physically abused by her husband in the camp, and he comes to her and promises to look after her always.

Rakeysh ji knew very well that I don't rehearse much, and that I like to do the shots as raw and impromptu as possible. We did do a few takes but something seemed amiss in the little boy's expressions. He seemed distracted and we didn't get what we'd wanted. After a few takes, taking account of the situation, Rakeysh ji calmly said, 'Okay, you guys have a cup of tea. Japtej and I will have a little chat.'

He held Japtej's hand and both of them went for a walk. From what I could overhear until they went out of sight was them discussing how cold it was. In ten minutes, they were back. And Rakeysh ji announced, '*Chalo ab shot lete hain* (Let's take the shot now).' He didn't say anything to either one of us and went straight for the take. I was expecting something to go amiss again, but the boy performed sheer magic. Absolutely transformed! Perfect take. I couldn't close my gaping mouth after the shot! What had happened in those ten minutes? To date, I have been most curious to know what he whispered in the child's ears that made him perform like a dream, but I never got to know.

Another very memorable instance from the same film was when we were shooting the very famous blazer scene between the brother and sister in Delhi. When Farhan and I went to rehearse, Rakeysh ji heard the scene from us and said, 'Okay, we have the scene, but give it your own beginning and end.' That got us thinking. I was casually dressed in jeans and top, and I sat on the floor to do some household chores, but something didn't feel right.

Rakeysh ji softly said, 'Divya, why don't you get into your costume and come back?'

That day, I realized the power of costumes and how they change your body language. The moment I came back, clad in salwar-kameez with the dupatta on my head, my stance and attitude changed. I automatically became apprehensive and unsure, like Isri Kaur should have been in the beginning of the scene. I sat in a certain way and began doing the chores as if it was my everyday routine. Farhan suggested that he would come wearing dark glasses and I added, 'Okay, then in that case, I won't recognize you.' So that became the beginning of our scene.

But we didn't have the end. Rakeysh ji came and said, 'Let's do it. You'll find it.'

I was wondering how I'd find it when we were getting into it without a clue as to how it would end, but on seeing Rakeysh ji, I let go of my thoughts and let Isri Kaur take over. The scene was going beautifully.

When Farhan gave me the earrings and I hugged him, I wondered again, as an actor, 'What next, now? How do we end the scene?' And then Isri Kaur came to my rescue.

That day, I learnt another very important thing—that the subconscious does not just belong to me, the person, but also to the role I play. So, as Isri, I suddenly remembered having seen our father salute the little Milkha—we had shot that scene in the previous schedule. On cue, I suddenly pulled myself out of the embrace and saluted the older Milkha.

That, for me, was the end of the scene, but I didn't hear a 'Cut' sound. When I couldn't hold the salute any longer, I looked at Rakeysh ji. He had tears in his eyes. Everyone was moist-eyed, and there was silence after the scene. Rakeysh ji came and hugged us. 'I told you, you'll find it.'

I had learnt a precious lesson that day, and I could only thank my director for teaching me, even without my realizing so, how to let the character take over the real me.

When we went to the vanity, I got chatting with Bharathi. 'You know something . . . ' she said, '. . . the characters you have played are very close to Rakeysh, as they are integral to his childhood. *Delhi-6*'s Jalebi was someone he had seen while growing up in the lanes of Chandni Chowk, and Isri Kaur has a huge reflection of his mother and him in his childhood.' That information was new to me. I already knew that those two roles were very special in my career, but that information made it even more precious. I could see how connected Rakeysh ji must have been to those roles, and I was lucky to have played both.

Bhaag Milkha Bhaag went on to become a super hit, and of course, it fetched me all the awards. But what it also got me was not just love, but reverence from the world over. I was flooded with messages, calls, letters, and social media posts from all parts of the world—everyone relating it to their childhoods and loving their sibling a little more. This film also changed the industry's perception of me.

In their terms, I had finally arrived.

I was no longer worried about being typecast. I had learnt from this amazing man when he had said, 'Just have a rollercoaster joyride with the role you play, and don't bother about the rest.'

I also realized that there are two kinds of filmmakers. The ones who replicate examples: going with tried and tested formulas, following the norms and set patterns, and then there are others who set examples for the world to follow. Rakeysh Mehra topped the list of the latter type for me, and I decided then that I would only work with directors who set examples.

One fine day, I went up to meet Rakeysh ji. I wanted to thank him for the landmark film he had given me. I sat there having my coffee and observing Rakeysh Mehra, the simple, humble man, one of the finest directors, who had taught me that acting didn't just happen with instructions—it is a journey that the actor and director undertake together to find that character and give it hues. I barely mustered a thank you. The silence did the rest.

But I surely want to say this. *This journey with you has been truly precious, Rakeysh ji. You made me meet myself, and enjoy the little pleasures; to witness the joy of now. You taught me to let go of 'me' when I took on a role, and let the role guide me. And yes, you taught this chatterbox the magic of silence. And if I could have my way, I'd like to continue this journey of discovering a variety of roles I wouldn't imagine myself in. Knowing you, you'll surely say, 'I know you'll do it.'*

When I say this, I can actually visualize him running his fingers through his hair silently, and then breaking the silence with a soft, 'Chalo karte hain ek acchi kahani, mazaa ayega (Let's do this great story, we'll have fun).'

GULZAR

I was at a press meet surrounded by journalists asking me questions. There was one question which got them the quickest reply from me, because for that, I did not have to think much. I knew the answer; my heart had known it for very long. 'Who is that one director you want to be directed by now?' one journalist asked. 'One and only—Gulzar saab,' was my instant reply.

Be it his movies or his poems, songs or short stories, or his silken voice reciting soulfully, for me, Gulzar saab has made my world a little more beautiful. I love the depth of his thoughts, of how simply he can weave magic with his words and express something so beautifully. You keep wondering how he romanticizes life and its situations so beautifully, that you can't help but fall in love with it. I have loved the poetic perspective he has towards everything, making even the most ordinary situations look extraordinary by finding a deeper hidden meaning and a hue which no one else has thought of.

I have read most of his books, devouring and savouring each word. All his recitals have been music to my ears. I have watched every film from *Mere Apne* to *Aandhi* and *Mausam*,

from *Angoor* to *Maachis* and then watched them all over
again. All those close to me know that I am a huge Gulzar
saab *mureed*.

Strangely, I only bumped into him a few times at events.
On such occasions, all you can say is a greeting. To start off
on how much you love someone's work without any context
would probably seem odd. So, I never got to say that to him.

One fine day, I got a call to moderate a newspaper launch
in Indore and before I could decline, the voice on the other
side said excitedly, 'Gulzar saab is coming and your chat will
be with him.'

'I am coming!' I blurted out before she could complete her
sentence. I called up my manager and told her to make sure
that there were no clashes on that particular date. I had to go!
I couldn't lose this chance of being *rubaroo* with Gulzar saab!

I reached Indore. As I sat sipping a cup of chai with the
organizers in the hotel lobby, I saw someone from the huge
glass window. Clad in crisp short white kurta and a pyjama,
walking barefoot on the grass: who else could it have been?

I asked the organizer when I could meet Gulzar saab to
discuss the flow of the event (all this while trying to contain
my excitement of getting to chat with him). He said he'd ask
Gulzar saab and let me know. As I got into my room, I was told,
'Gulzar saab abhi milna chahte hain (He wants to meet now).'
I quickly changed into a white crisp kurta-salwar to match his
(my way of showing solidarity). I was escorted to his suite.
While walking me there, I was asked if I knew of Gulzar saab's
works, so it could be easy to have a discussion. I just smiled
within. Only if they knew!

As they opened the door, I saw him. Him in that white
kurta-pyjama and a warm smile. He greeted me with an *adaab*
in that mesmerizing voice of his, and I did the same. I didn't

feel as if I was meeting him properly for the first time. I wasn't awkward or inhibited at all. Having grown on his works, I had a sense of comfort and familiarity. And I chose to just speak my heart, no holds barred.

So, my talkative self was out there. Seeing the man whose words had given me the depth and intensity to see the world differently, I couldn't hold myself back. It was like meeting a long-lost dear one. And I started, 'Gulzar saab, *adaab*. The organizers wanted to make sure I know of your works. I know each and every one.' And I started discussing anecdotes with him. His films, his poetry, his recitals; I was on a roll. He looked amused and a bit surprised too. '*Arey! Tum toh sab jaanti ho* (You know everything),' he said affectionately, as if talking to a little child, indulging me as I went on and on.

The organizers looked dumbfounded, but my chatter didn't stop. The organizer then finally intervened. 'Ma'am, can we talk about the flow of the show?'

Before I could say anything, Gulzar saab protectively answered, '*Kya discuss karna hai, bacchi toh sab janti hai. Bas stage pe guppein maarenge* (What's there to discuss? She knows everything. We'll just chat on stage).'

I had a huge grin on my face at his warm and affectionate stance towards me. I don't know how I had sounded blurting out all that I had wanted to say to someone I always wanted to meet. I was beaming and felt that my genuine fondness for him had reached the sensitive man. I had seen his attitude change from being quiet to totally at ease. I was really happy.

In the evening, I was escorted to the huge venue, thronging with people, all waiting to hear Gulzar saab. The hosts told me, 'At the end of your session, please ensure that Gulzar saab also speaks about the newspaper. Please mark it on your flow chart, Ma'am.' I think after their experience of seeing me get carried away with my chatter about Gulzar saab, they just wanted to remind me sweetly but surely about not forgetting the topic of the evening. For a change, I had not prepared a flow chart. With him, I wanted to go with the flow—his song lyrics, '*Katra katra milti hai . . . Katra katra jeene do . . . Zindagi hai, zindagi hai . . . Behne do, behne do . . .,*' reverberating within. Yes, I wanted life to flow in his magical presence, and that surely couldn't be planned.

As I sat down to chat with him, I must admit I was a bit nervous. But he put me at ease with his warmth, beginning the conversation with some lovely words for me. I could gauge that he trusted me to do it well and was very comfortable. Within seconds, we started discussing his poetry and eventually touched upon all topics—life, relationships, love, everything.

His voice was music to the ears. He was enjoying sharing some of his most beautiful lines, memories and anecdotes too. The audience kept asking for more. I wanted to go on listening to him and in the process, we exceeded our allotted time. *Who likes to be bound by time when discussing poetry with Gulzar saab?*

A girl came up with a chit for me—I was sure it was a reminder to finally get talking about the newspaper, but before she could reach me, Gulzar saab protectively said, '*Arey bhai mazaa aa raha hai baatein kar ke, akhbaar ki baat bhi karenge, iss parchi ki zaroorat nahin hai* (We are having a good time, we'll talk about the newspaper too, this chit is not needed).' Everyone in the audience, including the organizers, had a hearty laugh. It didn't seem like a formal inaugural event at all. Gulzar saab was really enjoying himself, and I was on cloud nine. It was a special day.

As we got off the stage, the same organizer walked towards me, beaming. 'God! You both complemented each other so well! Gulzar saab was so relaxed and seemed to really enjoy himself.

We had a great session. Thank you!' As we left, Gulzar saab asked me and my colleague Hema, who also handles PR for me, '*Khaana khaogi mere saath?* (Will you have dinner with me?)'

'Of course, Gulzar saab!' both of us said in unison.

In his august presence, along with his friend, we chatted nineteen to the dozen. For me, the best time was talking to him in Punjabi, and hearing him respond in Punjabi too. I totally felt at home with my most favourite person—telling him about myself, home, Ma, films and how it was my biggest desire to be directed by him. He was all smiles, listening to me patiently. That surely was an evening to remember.

The next morning, we were all to board the same flight back to Mumbai. As Hema and I reached the airport, Gulzar saab was already seated in the VIP lounge with his friend and the organizer. He saw me, and gestured to me to sit next to him, warmly saying, '*Ye bacchi bahut pyaari hai* (This kid is lovely).'

It overwhelmed me. I felt this sense of belonging, of having somebody looking over, especially the one you have looked up to all your life. It's not an ordinary feeling for an emotional woman like me. We chatted a bit more and then the usher walked in, 'The flight is ready to board.' Gulzar saab and his friend briskly walked towards the escalator. I couldn't keep up with his speed and was left behind. I think he realized that I was not with them and he turned back to look for me from the escalator. I was running to catch up with him. He protectively extended his hand, like a father extending a hand to his child and affectionately said, '*Aaja beta!* (Come on child!)'

Those words that day fulfilled a thousand desires of the child within me, to be held securely and to make sure I don't fall. He sensed it too and said, 'One, two, three . . .' as if guiding a little child to take that leap of faith on the count of three. As if on cue, and just like a little child, I jumped off the escalator holding his hand tightly, and literally clapped, not just for having finally jumped off safely but because those few seconds had satiated my child-like desire to be treated as such. And I clapped and laughed for very long, I guess. And it's embedded in my heart forever.

So that was Gulzar saab and my unforgettable meeting with him. And that day, the bond strengthened for me, the connect now was far deeper. We didn't exchange numbers, but email IDs. After all, *khat likhna* (writing letters) is much more beautiful when it is Gulzar saab.

I keep writing to him and his replies are cherished. The last one says, in Punjabi, '*Jee ayaan nu* (most welcome) *Covid se fursat milei to milein.*'

Ji of course, dil dhoondta hai phir wahi, fursat ke raat din and another memorable meeting with the inimitable Gulzar saab.

SHABANA AZMI

The doorbell rang and a packet was delivered to my house. My house help duly delivered it to me saying, '*Didi, aapka birthday gift Shabana ji ke yahan se aaya hai* (Your birthday gift has come from Shabana ji's place).' In these unusual times amidst the pandemic, my birthday had been a low-key affair—just two of my besties and the neighbourhood friends of my little niece and nephew had come.

In such times, meeting them too seemed like such a blessing. So, amidst lots of laughter and chatter, I opened the packet, and out came a stunning saree. There was something extremely classy about it. Had to be—it was from Shabana Azmi, who is a classy woman. Every which way.

I couldn't help but gasp, and I could hear oohs and wows from my friends too. Along with the saree was a small envelope which read, 'From Shabana and Javed'.

I couldn't wait to read what was written in the note. These little notes always matter to me, conveying all the love and warmth along with the gift, and there is always a sense of curiosity to know what the person has written for you.

Well, I knew there would be something special jotted down in that card, but I wasn't prepared for what I read. 'Dear Divya, you are very special to me and hence, I know you will cherish my mother's saree that I am sending for you.'

I read it again and then again, and a few more times, until I could not read any more as tears blurred my eyes. I tried to absorb each word written in there, and the enormity of what they conveyed. That was quite a gesture, and she would only have done it for someone who meant a lot to her.

To be loved like this is a blessing. I held the note close to my heart for a few seconds. It was from someone I loved the most too. Yes, over the years, Shabana Azmi has become an integral part of my life. Isn't it amazing that life has taken its dream course for me? She is someone I grew up watching and adoring as an actor, and I not only got to work with one of the finest actors we have, but am also lucky enough to have a strong bond with her.

In school, during the recess, we were discussing favourite actors. I instantly said Amitabh Bachchan and Shabana Azmi. The little me was amazed to see this actor as a glamorous heroine in my favourite films like *Amar Akbar Anthony* and *Parvarish*. The same heroine had played a variety of strong, female-centric roles in *Arth*, *Mandi*, *Nishant*, and then also feel-good films like *Swami*. She did them all with such finesse! Whichever film she did, she looked like she belonged there. I wanted to be like her, even in school. And even later. Even now. And even while I write this.

I love the way she's balanced her life, not only professionally, but also with her friendships, work associations, her philosophies and her emotions. I sometimes really wish I was like her. Whenever I look at her, what's most striking about her is her zest for life.

I met her first on the sets of *Umrao Jaan*, where she was reprising the role her mother Shaukat Azmi had played in the original. And I was playing her daughter. That was one of the main reasons I had said yes to the film apart from the fact that it was a J.P. Dutta film.

We were in Jaipur, shooting at the exotic City Palace. I was there with my mother. It was a few days of wait before I could shoot with Shabana Azmi. My first shot with her was in the palace itself, which was converted into a courtyard set. In the scene, I was supposed to be dancing on a classical number, and she, as my mother, was right in front of me, watching me, to judge if I was a good enough dancer to be the main courtesan. To say I was nervous was an understatement. I was finally meeting my most favourite actor, playing her daughter, and dancing in front of her very experienced and skilful gaze.

Shabana Azmi has a very enigmatic and mesmerizing presence. You can't help but be intimidated by her, especially when you are being introduced. I cleared my throat, and mentally prepared myself to introduce myself formally.

I was all too conscious when I said, 'Hi Shabana ji, I am Divya Dutta.'

She looked up and responded with a pleasant 'Hi'. Her twinkling eyes held a tinge of mischief, but there was something about her which made me feel that she was a very no-nonsense and strict person. But I was sure I saw a naughty glint.

'So, you are playing my daughter?' she asked casually.

'Ji.' I couldn't say more.

'Prepared with your dance steps?' she asked, half-smiling, but I was still nervous.

'Ji, I think so.'

'Good. All the best.'

Pause.

I ran back to the comfort of my corner, and requested the choreographer to take me through the steps again. I didn't want to goof up in front of Shabana ji, otherwise my first impression would be ruined.

When the shot was ready, J.P. Dutta said, 'Action,' and I started dancing. I tried not to look at her (which I should have) and get enamoured. I heard a 'Cut' sound in between my sequence. *Gosh! Had I goofed up?* Thankfully, it was a technical error. As I heard 'Action' again, I started dancing. This time, I managed to steal a glance at her. Yes, she was looking at me, intently at that. I quickly looked away, lest I faltered.

The shot was okayed. As I was about to go back to my seat, I heard someone call out my name. Yes, it was her! My heart skipped a beat as I quickly ran towards her. '*Shabash! Bahut accha kiya,*' she said warmly. I smiled. My heart was still fluttering inside. 'Are you trained?'

'Ji. My *maasi* is a dance lecturer in Punjab. I learnt from her.' In my enthusiasm, I murmured, '. . . and in school, Shabana ji, you were my . . .' and I gulped the words. I couldn't complete my story of her being my most favourite of them all. Actually, I wouldn't blame myself for that! I was trying to grasp a lot of stuff, the biggest of them being that I had actually performed in front of Shabana Azmi and shared screen space with her! I had a smile on my face and stood there looking at her, wanting to say a lot and ending up saying nothing.

I saw that glint in her eyes and she smiled and said, '*Jao, daudo ab* (Run along).'

I ran like a child, straight into my vanity van, to the comfort of my Ma, who was waiting there. I plonked myself on her lap. 'Ma, you know, it went so well! Shabana ji patted me!' Ma was thrilled. 'Arey, I would have loved to see you give your first shot with your favourite actor, *par tune aane hi nahi diya* (You didn't let me come).'

I had strictly told Ma not to be there on the set as all my attention would then be on her and what she thought of my performance. So, I had kept her away, but I gave her a scene-by-scene description. She was laughing on seeing my child-like enthusiasm. After a few days, I took Ma on a night shoot to the palace. I wanted to introduce her to Shabana ji. I still can't find words to express how it felt to have Ma meet my idol. They exchanged pleasantries as I introduced them. But I was still a bit formal. And I did not miss that glint in her eyes again.

In between shots, we had some time, and instead of dispersing to our respective rooms and vanity vans, we all decided to stay on the set. It was a cold winter night. My spot boy got me my blanket-like shawl which was dull in colour but very warm. As he wrapped it around me, I heard Shabana ji say, 'What's that you are wrapping around you?'

'It's a shawl, Shabana ji,' I said proudly and just as I was about to tell her where I had bought it from, I heard her say, '*Yeh kis type ka shawl hai?* (What type of a shawl is this?) A challenge to the aesthetics.'

I stopped myself from sharing any further details. She clearly looked very amused. That glint was a little more obvious.

I ran up to my mother who was chatting with another actor and whispered in her ear, 'Mumma, give me your shawl na, you take mine. This looks like a blanket.' Well, moms don't ask, so she didn't. She gave me her beautiful shawl and I wrapped it around myself and ran back to the set. If Shabana ji had noticed, she didn't say, but she certainly looked very amused.

Everyone seemed to be doing their own thing when Shabana ji announced, '*Chalo*, let's play dumb charades till the shot is ready.' Who would say no to the charming woman's suggestion? So, Abhishek Bachchan and Shabana ji were in one team, and

Aishwarya Rai Bachchan and I in the other. The game went on in full swing, and I saw Shabana ji taking charge and making sure everyone was involved and having fun. She was laughing, joking and cheering everyone up, and I saw a different side of her: the absolute fun-loving side.

It was finally my turn, and I was given a tough film title. My team guessed it quickly, and I heard a cheering sound from the rival team. '*Bahut achche!*' she shouted out from the other side. I have observed that she always admires and acknowledges what she likes and doesn't hold back. And, of course, that means a lot to whoever it is for. Needless to say, I was elated. Many such games ensued, and I became more comfortable in her company. I could now have a conversation with her without being utterly self-conscious.

She was a picture of perfection on the set. Even if it wasn't my shot, I would be on the set to see her perform. She would be engrossed in her role, feeling her character. Her passion towards her craft was very obvious, and she was an absolutely different person in front of the camera. As many times as she rehearsed for the shot, she put in as much emotion as the previous one. Not a single 'being out of it for a bit' casual moment.

As I watched her, I realized that I couldn't do too many rehearsals. I tend to become mechanical after each rehearsal. So, I wanted to see how she was a master at being as fresh and passionate with each passing shot. I would see her discuss the nuances and understand the scene from the director's point of view and give it her own nuances too. Every shot was like it was her first shot.

When she was called for a big monologue, she calmly went in front of the camera. I wondered, 'Didn't she want to rehearse all those lines?' (Because I hadn't seen her do it on set). She had the script, but she wasn't reading it. She wasn't looking at anyone, she was somewhere else. As the director said, 'Action,' she transported me to her world. Out poured the impeccable lines, with nuances, and the pauses she wanted.

Everyone stood spellbound. That was a perfect single shot. After the director shouted 'Cut', everyone applauded. I stood there gazing at the woman who had won three consecutive National Awards. I could see her love for her work, her dedication towards it. She had come so well-prepared on set that she didn't need to see the dialogue sheets again. I stood there, besotted. Like everyone else.

After we wrapped up the shoot, I wondered sadly when I'd see her again.

And then work and the buzzing city of Mumbai took over.

Just before Holi, I got a message. 'Join us to celebrate Holi. Shaukat Azmi, Shabana, Javed, Baba Azmi and Tanvi.'

I was ecstatic! I had been invited by her! I was going to meet her again! And that too, at her very popular and much-talked about Holi celebration. It felt nice that she had personally invited me. She has that *apnapan,* that warmth which is so evident.

I had emptied my closet, looking for the best white outfits I had. I did want to make a statement, a good one at that, and wash away any doubts she had about my dressing sense after the grand fiasco of having been seen wrapped in my blanket-shawl. I knew she probably wouldn't say it but she'd most definitely notice and observe. And I had, by now, realized she had a keen eye for aesthetics.

That was the first time I was going to lay my foot in Shaukat aapa and Kaifi saab's very popular bungalow at Janki Kutir, which was famous for housing many budding talents and for creative mehfils and celebrations. I dressed up like Chandni—

in all white with oxidized jewellery, and colourful bangles, and entered the gates, holding my mother's hand. The house reflected the tastes of its residents: classy, simple and welcoming. The who's who of the industry were already there but my eyes were looking for her.

Amid the dry colours that were being thrown all around, I saw the one whose vibrance outshone all the other colours around her. She was laughing and chatting with all those who had gathered around her. Dressed in a sleek, white kurta-salwar, she had covered her head with a colourful dupatta tied stylishly like a turban. She didn't say hi to me, just pulled Ma and me to the dance floor, applied gulaal and asked what we'd like to have. In no time, I was comfortable, rather, I felt at home. Ma made friends with a few ladies soon and got busy with them. I too went and met all those familiar to me. Then I stood in a corner with my drink when I saw Shabana ji gesturing from a distance, asking me to join her. 'Come, we are taking a group picture,' she said enthusiastically. All the female actors stood around her and clicked some fun pictures in an *adaab* pose as guided by her!

It's always very festive and fun to be around her, never a dull moment. She makes sure that life and every moment of it is lived to the fullest. She introduced my mother and me to Javed saab (to whom I have dedicated a separate chapter) and to Shaukat aapa—I hit it off with both instantly.

By the time I left Janki Kutir, I had also left behind my apprehensions and awkwardness. Ma said smilingly, 'They feel like family.'

Yes, they did. And eventually, they became one, thanks to Shabana ji who always made an effort. *How many people actually do that? Especially super successful and super busy people. How many of them just take a moment and do that special something that would mean a lot to someone else?*

But Shabana Azmi always does—bringing smiles to people around her and in the process, having those people love her and becoming friends for life.

* * *

One day, on an outdoor shoot in a far-flung village in Rajasthan, where one had to stand in a certain place at a certain angle to get network and make calls, I sat sulking. The reason was that I was unable to join my *Delhi-6* team for the premiere in Delhi because there were no direct flights from there and it would take three days for me to go and come back. I couldn't possibly have the entire unit waiting as all the scenes we were shooting then required my presence. Ma had pacified me with her pep talk, but I was still sulking. It was a special film for me, and I'd miss watching it with my team.

I was cribbing in my head when the mobile rang. The name that flashed took me by surprise. I picked up the phone and ran out to stand on the water tank of the four-room hotel. I didn't want to miss that call! 'Hello Shabana ji!' I shouted at the top of my voice, making sure she could hear me.

'*Kya kaam kiya hai, Divya*! (What fabulous work you have done!) *Mashallah*! I had to call you,' she said excitedly. It didn't register what exactly she was talking about. I wondered even amidst all the excitement of getting a call from her. '*Ye lo, baat karo*,' she said handing over the phone to someone. I was still confused when I heard the other female voice, '*Bhai, kitna umda kaam kiya tumne, mujhe laga sach mein Delhi-6 se hi koi ladki le aye hain! Jeeti raho!* (You have done a great job, I felt as if they actually brought in somebody from Delhi-6 to do the role! God bless you with a long life!)'

Now it all fell into place, and I slowly absorbed what had just been said to me. It was not a small thing that Shaukat aapa herself had praised me—a prolific actor and theatre veteran like her saying all that made me euphoric. If I could dance on that water tank I was standing on, I would have. But the busy market below and people gazing at the actor who was stuck between the ladder and the water tank, refrained me from doing so. I was on top of the world (literally)! I don't remember how many times I said 'thank you' to aapa.

'*Yeh lo, Shabana se baat karo.*' And I heard her vibrant voice again, '*Abhi nikle theatre se* Delhi-6 *ka preview dekh kar. Shabash, khush raho*!' and she hung up.

And I hung on to that ladder for a few more minutes, swinging and laughing. In my heart, the song '*Panchi Banun Udti Phirun*' (I feel like transforming into a bird and flying)' kept playing on a loop. Shabana ji and Shaukat aapa had more than made up for my absence at the premiere. Shabana ji, once again, proving the fact that if she likes something, she appreciates and acknowledges it—she never forgets. My first calls for reviews on a film have always been from Shabana Azmi, and then Javed saab takes the phone. It has become a ritual now and it's my tonic. It just rejuvenates and enthuses me.

Those little gestures, those moments that are made so special, are what made me see her very sensitive side. On the set, she's always the diva—professional and into her role. And off-screen, in a happy comfortable atmosphere, she's the life of the gathering with her anecdotes, her superb wit and her child-like exuberance, and not to forget, that naughty glint in her eyes.

Shabana ji and Javed saab's house became home soon. I would be there for all special occasions. We have a group of young actors including Konkona Sen Sharma, Tannishtha Chatterjee, Dia Mirza, Shahana Goswami, Sandhya Mridul,

Vidya Balan and I must say, that in spirit, the youngest of us all is Shabana Azmi. I'll never forget an all-girl eve we had, where we were chatting away like friends, laughing over everything, reminiscing and recounting incidents. And Shabana ji was the one having the most fun. All of us girls in her house, the child in each one having a ball of a time, playing games, and indulging in girly chat. I saw in her, once again, that someone who knew how to make the most of life, who moulded herself every time according to the given situation and didn't hold herself back from enjoying any moment to the fullest.

For me, that has been a big takeaway for life.

I have also seen Shabana Azmi weave her magic on stage. Be it in *Tumhari Amrita* where she, as Amrita Nigam and Farooq Shaikh as Zulfi, read letters written to one another, narrating their life's journey with and without each other—a poignant story of love or any of her other plays like, *Kaifi Aur Main* and *Broken Images*, I have loved watching her perform! But I just couldn't get *Tumhari Amrita* out of my head. How effortlessly she would become child-like while reading one letter, and then, in the next moment, turn vivacious, and then suddenly, a tear would trickle out of her eye while feeling the pain and loneliness. How brilliantly she had gotten into the skin of that role, playing Amrita for a good twenty-two years. I remain mesmerized!

I always thought that if I ever perform on stage, it would be something like *Tumhari Amrita*. And when you really wish for something with all your heart, even the universe conspires to make it happen. One fine day, I got a call from Om Puri. He asked me in his distinct baritone voice in Punjabi, '*Play karengi mere naal? Main* Tumhari Amrita *da Punjabi version bana reha haan!*'

He had asked me if I wanted to do the Punjabi version of *Tumhari Amrita*! That, for me, was a double delight! *Tumhari*

Amrita, my dream role, in Punjabi, and that too with Om Puri. I was ecstatic! But I did want to share this with Shabana ji. It was only ethical to share it with someone who had lived that role for so many years! So, I went to her house to share this news with her and I wasn't sure how she'd feel about it. I was apprehensive. I didn't know how to begin the conversation. One thing that I find very interesting about Shabana ji is that she never greets with a regular, 'Hi, how are you?' She always begins as if we are already in the midst of a conversation. It always sets the mood for the meeting. It warms up the person she wants to chat with immediately.

She came into the living room, as always, full of life. After a bit, I brought out the reason why I was visiting her. She was very casual about it, and said, 'Well, that's wonderful. Divya! I'm so happy.' I was surprised, and a bit taken aback. I probably wouldn't have reacted like that. I think I am possessive about the roles I play. But she had shown immense large-heartedness and grace, and she was genuinely happy.

She just asked me who was directing it and then the conversation changed to another topic. We were laughing and chatting about everything else. She had made it that simple with her magnanimity. As I was leaving, I told her that it would mean a lot if she came for the premiere night and she promised she would. 'I'll be there to cheer you!'

My heart was full when I got into my car. This dynamic actor loved to see everyone around her spread their wings, and with her encouragement and motivation, she made the skies delightful to fly in.

On the opening night, I was nervous as hell. The who's who had come to watch the play. How could I be half as good as her? And would she even come? A million thoughts crossed my mind. My heart was pounding so much, it could have just popped out of my chest. All I wanted to do was run back home and sleep, and shut myself from all this nervous tension. But just then, the curtains were raised, and I saw the audience. In the front row sat the one person who I really wanted there at that time; cheering me on: Shabana Azmi.

I could hear her cheering us up. It lifted my spirits and my confidence. I had to perform well. This would be my tribute to my most favourite of them all. I just shut my eyes to recall the impact that all the gamut of emotions I had seen Shabana ji portray when she played Amrita had on me. I was all set to give it my own, my all. It felt like a breeze after that. I realized, it is so important, along with your hard work and effort, to be inspired, encouraged and motivated. Something that sounds tough to achieve. You try to push the envelope for that one person watching you (of course, along with a gallery of others). It always happened to me in Shabana ji's presence. The fact that she was watching me always made me up my quotient, whether it was my dressing style or my performance.

After the play got over, and we got standing ovations, the voice I heard distinctly was hers. And she was so excited and happy that she came up on stage to wish Om ji and me, and speak about us. I had shut my eyes because had I opened them, tears would have rolled out. In my head, I could hear the voice from my childhood, 'You know how Shabana Azmi does everything with perfection, I want to be like her!' That voice now mingled and merged with hers as I stood on stage hearing her generous words for us. Life, that day, had come full circle. My feeling of fondness and admiration for her reached another level as she held my hand and lifted it in the air. That day, I fell in love with Shabana Azmi a little more, for being the person that she is.

As I mentioned, when you really want something, the universe makes it happen. I got the golden opportunity to work with Shabana ji again, this time, playing the antagonist in a film based on teachers called *Chalk and Duster*.

I saw the lovely jodi of Shabana Azmi and the late Girish Karnad coming together again after the very memorable *Swami*. I was playing the bad gal. Though I was super excited about sharing screen space with Shabana ji again, I was wondering how I'd act nasty in front of her, a similar feeling that I had experienced while doing *Baghban* with Mr Bachchan years ago.

The scene was a face-off between Shabana ji and me. To be honest, I was on my toes. I knew that along with playing her part exceptionally well, she'd be watching me. And I had to do well too, to not let her down. I had improved my skills in mostly everything, knowing that she was watching. I had learnt to mix and match my clothes from her. Whatever she wore, it looked stylish. She'd just dismiss compliments by saying, 'I just took that blouse and matched it with this saree and just added a drape and some complementing jewellery.' But how lovely that combination would look!

I started doing that too. It kind of made me feel liberated— not sticking to the usual, regular matched stuff, taking risks, breaking patterns, experimenting and being confident that I could carry it off. All this had come from her.

And here I was, standing in front of her for a face-off. I was sure she knew I was tense, because while doing the rehearsal, she had held my hand warmly, without saying anything. That eased me completely. She's all affection and warmth, and does it so breezily that you take a while to even realize it. And of course, that's extremely heartwarming.

It was supposed to be a trolley shot. The camera was in the capable hands of ace cinematographer and Shabana ji's brother, Baba Azmi (one of the most genuine persons I know). It was with both of us actors in profile, and the camera in the centre. By then, I did know my camera angles, but obviously, with Shabana ji in front of me, my focus was only on her. I was so engrossed in rehearsing with her that I didn't realize that instead of my profile, I was standing with my back to the camera. Shabana ji, while speaking her lines, subtly moved forward and physically turned me towards the camera.

I could hear a chuckle from both the lovely siblings. 'Show your face, my dear,' she said. I managed a smile. I was hating mouthing mean lines to her, but she was so in her role that I couldn't help but forget my personal equation and play the mean part with gusto. On seeing her in front of me—absolutely immersed in her part—I went all out with mine too!

That's what they call being inspired by someone, I guess. The saying that acting is all about reacting couldn't have been more applicable as it was in this situation. I was not speaking the dialogues now, but reacting to her expressions, her lines. With the modulations in her voice and body language, I was automatically changing mine and instead of being tense, I was thoroughly enjoying it.

That's the joy of working with an actor of her calibre. The situation felt so real because of her involvement in it that I felt we were living that moment. Even on screen, I think living the moment is a given with Shabana Azmi.

I had closely been observing Shabana Azmi, the daughter, the wife, the sister, sister-in-law, and a friend too—and she was all love. I think her mantra is to spread love and happiness around. Be it taking her father Kaifi saab's Mijwan Welfare Society, which is very close to his heart, to every nook and corner of the country and abroad, or celebrating his birth anniversary along with Baba sir at Janki Kutir every year by inviting budding as well as established poets and writers to recite their work, or publishing Shaukat aapa's book, *Kaifi and I*, and then performing it on stage with Javed saab, to being the best friend of her brother and sister-in-law, or a go-to friend for all her close friends, she does it all.

What a fantabulous journey of a doting daughter celebrating her legendary parents as a way of life! Once, while driving back together, she was narrating Kaifi saab's anecdotes to me, and she told me he endearingly called his *ladali* beti 'Chidiya'. Rightly so. He gave her the wings to fly.

With her and Javed saab, I always thought what they have is a dream bond. They have always been the best of friends, sharing their love for poetry, literature, social causes they strongly believe in, and standing firmly together with laughter, jokes, fun, celebration, and above all, a strong emotional bond which is always apparent in everything they do. Once on a flight, I had told Shabana ji to find a good match for me, and she had burst into naughty laughter. 'Never ask me that. My track record of matchmaking is disastrous!'

But she always knows what is happening in my life. I've always gone to her to seek advice on anything and everything, and her advice has always been practical: accepting the situation and moving ahead with solutions. She doesn't believe in crying over spilt milk. She's always guided me to mop the floor and get a new glass of milk, always looking ahead in life to newer possibilities and changes. I love her attitude towards life. Ma would also tell me the same, but emotional chaos has always been a part of my life. I get so carried away by situations that it takes me a while to get out of them. On seeing her, I realized life shouldn't be taken that seriously—give the situation its due importance, absorb it and let it go. Pick yourself up and out of it and move on: the best way of self-preservation.

When Ma passed away, Shabana ji was one of the first people I called. 'She's gone.' And Shabana ji and Javed saab were home with me in no time, holding me up through the toughest phase of my life. Then, when I wrote my book, *Me and Ma*, to celebrate my mother and express my gratitude as a very lucky daughter, for the foreword, I could just think of Shabana ji because of the doting daughter that she is. Bas, I went up to her one day and told her about the book, and that the book would get a strong foundation if she wrote the foreword. We were at an event, so she quickly told me before getting into her car, 'Send me the manuscript.'

I waited eagerly to hear from her. I was home when I got a text message from her. 'Your foreword will be ready in a week.' I was elated. And had she been around me, I would have hugged her tightly and told her how much it meant to me that she was writing it. When I got the mail and read her foreword, I marvelled at how articulately she had described my relationship with Ma. Well, I was overwhelmed, but not surprised. All her strength and sensitivity as a human being was apparent in her writing for me. I had hugged the mobile for a bit. I called and thanked her. 'Wish you good luck as I may not be in town during the launch, but I have read the book and love it.' She never minces words, says them as it should be said—no layering.

* * *

I was on the top of the world when my director friend, Faraz Ansari, came to me with an LGBTQ story and then said, 'Divya, how I wish we get Shabana ji to play your mother. It would be lethal!' For me, it meant a lot more to play her daughter again, after *Umrao Jaan*. But this time, it would be different. My bond with Shabana ji had become truly special. I wouldn't even have to make an effort when I had to say my lines in front of her. It would flow naturally for me. Acting, as I always say, is mostly about reacting. I was more excited than Faraz, and I immediately sent a message to Shabana ji.

The wait ended for both of us when Faraz excitedly called me. 'DD, Shabana ji said yes!' I actually enjoyed the little suspense and then the good news. It's like waiting for an exam result and then getting to know that you haven't just passed but have topped the charts.

Shabana ji, Swara Bhasker (another super talented actor who plays my partner in this film) and I got together for a reading with Faraz at a five-star hotel. The rest of us sat across the table and read the lines, joking and chatting in between too, while waiting for Shabana ji, who was giving an interview.

As soon as she came and sat for the rehearsal, the atmosphere of the reading session totally changed. Earlier, we were just reading our lines, but the moment she spoke, it was with full emotion. I could feel everyone's body language change. We all straightened up. The jovial mood flew out of the huge window of the five-star suite, and automatically, Swara and I were speaking our dialogues in the same mood as her. There was only professionalism at that table. Discussions, improvisations—everything happened.

I'll never forget her gesture on the sets of *Sheer Qorma*. We were doing a highly emotional breakdown scene between mother and daughter, and we had rehearsed the lines once. Just then, Faraz called, 'Come DD, let's rehearse again with Shabana ji.' I quickly got up and went. I spoke a line and then it was a big dialogue from Shabana ji followed by mine. She spoke her lines with full emotion. Watching her, I was going to start my big dialogue with full emotion too, but she placed her hand on my mouth. 'Shhhh! Keep your magic for the shot!' she whispered.

I could have broken down right there! How sensitive was she! She had remembered that I get mechanical with rehearsals, and how generous of her to let me keep my best for the shot! How many people do that: caring for the scene as a whole, including the co-actor's performance and not just their own? How many, really?

Somewhere along the way, I got extremely attached to her. Meeting her often, those lovely girly get-togethers with the gang, clicking pictures in the adaab pose, sharing my highs and lows with her, and taking advice—everything was special. And she has continued the tradition of calling me, along with Javed saab, every time she sees my latest performance. I really consider myself very lucky for this amazing bond I have with Shabana ji. She always insists, 'Call me Shabana!' I just can't get myself to do that ever.

One day, I heard Shaukat aapa had passed. I knew Shabana ji would be devastated—she loved Shaukat aapa so very much! I remembered watching videos of them singing fun songs and laughing together. It reminded me of my own fun bond with Ma. So similar . . .

I immediately went to see her. Shaukat aapa was adorned with beautiful flowers, as everyone sought their last darshan of her. Shabana ji looked quiet, in control of her emotions as well as the situation. She had taken charge of giving her mother the tribute she deserved. When I hugged her, she quietly plucked a flower from a pot on the table and put it in my hair. That gesture said a lot to me—of Shaukat aapa's love for flowers and of her affection for me. It symbolized the love flowing to me from both these majestic women. I kept that flower with me.

The next day, the lovely daughter gave her legendary mother a befitting tribute, and stood tall, in control of everything.

Pride for her mother was written all over her face and she took everyone's tributes and condolences very gracefully. She celebrated her mother with the world—a life beautifully lived deserved just that.

* * *

One fine day, I got a call from her. '*Accha, toh Jaadu jo hain, wo 75 ke ho rahe hain* (Jaadu is turning seventy-five) and we are all throwing a Bollywood-themed party. *Tum kya banogi?* (What will you come as?)' I went as Meena Kumari from *Pakeezah*, and saw Shabana ji dressed in polka dots along with the birthday boy.

She was like an exuberant child, full of excitement to celebrate her 'Jaadu's' birthday. Naughty, full-of-life, dancing, making everyone dance along with her on Bollywood numbers, cracking jokes and laughing. I just watched her. People loved to be around her, maybe just to feel that energy too, and yes, everyone was in full form.

The next day was the big gala dinner at a five-star where the entire industry was invited. It was a big party and I went looking for Javed saab and Shabana ji. I saw Javed saab and went and wished him. Then he pointed in a certain direction and said, '*Shabana udhar hai shayad, mil lo.*' She was standing in a corner with a few guests and looked stunning. I went and met her. There was a glow on her face, of happiness, and of love, of course. She met me warmly and then got busy with other guests. After a few hours, I felt a strange restlessness and thought it best to probably leave. Very strangely, I had this desperate urge to meet her, and my eyes looked around for her to say goodbye. Finally, I found her on the dance floor, and I don't know why I hugged her tight.

'When are you back? I want to sit and chat with you,' I blurted out, like a child.

She said enthusiastically, 'Tomorrow, I leave for Khandala to our bungalow. You see Jaadu's celebrations are still on. I'll see you when I am back.'

I was still restless. The next afternoon, I got a call from a journalist. 'So, what do you have to say about Shabana ji?'

I was confused. 'What about her? I met her yesterday and . . .'

He interrupted me. 'You don't know, Ma'am? Shabana ji met with an accident on her way to Khandala.'

My little world came crumbling down. In those few moments, it hit me how much Shabana Azmi meant to me. I was numb. 'They have rushed her to the hospital.' I was shaken. But something inside nudged me. 'Don't you know her zest for life? And don't you know life loves her just as much! How many people, after all, know how to live it? She does. And she'll fight it to get back to it in full form, since she is the best student of life.'

I prayed, I called everyone, and finally amidst the strict rules from the very protective—and rightly so—Tanvi (as there was a crowd of people wanting to visit her), I got a green signal to quickly meet her. 'I want her to rest, otherwise she starts chatting!' Tanvi said.

It brought a smile to my face. My lovely, adorable Shabana ji. I quietly tiptoed into her room, and I saw the doctor talking to her. She saw me and smiled warmly. If she had her way, she would have started talking, mid-conversation.

She gestured slowly for me to enter, but I stood at the door and waved, indicating that I'd see her later at home soon. Back home, when I went to visit her, I was expecting a serious atmosphere, but was pleasantly surprised. Shabana ji sat with a brace around her neck, joking and laughing with Javed saab,

Farhan and the others. Yes, she was back, and so was the life of the house!

I felt so happy to meet her. There were no discussions on the accident or pain or suffering. Like any other normal day, she was discussing films, history, etc., and I just looked at her, amazed. She wanted it that way—leaving the incident behind her, and celebrating life again. I wondered—how long and how many times do we tend to rewind an incident and discuss what happened, and here was a woman, laughing through the pain and showing the world how it's done.

After that, I left for my outdoor shoots and then the sudden lockdown was announced. It had been so many months and I hadn't seen her. Finally, after the lockdown was eased, I visited her and Javed saab at their bungalow in Khandala, and with the entire family there, it seemed so full of life again.

We played dumb charades, and there was a delicious lunch. Then Shabana ji said she was going to take an improvisation class for Asha Bhosle ji's granddaughter as she had been requested, and I just promptly asked, 'Why should I miss being taught by you?'

Not a moment was wasted. 'Come then, join!' The three of us did an improvisation session. I was doing that after so many years since my acting class. I was absorbing and cherishing each moment and learning from her.

When I left, looking at her from the rear-view mirror, I was emotional. That figure I was leaving behind, of a magnificent woman, got blurred as the car moved ahead. How happy I was to see her, how happy I was to know her, how happy I was to peep into her beautiful world. Yes, she is family to me, and a teacher, and my favourite.

And here I was at home, hugging that note from Shabana ji and that saree. This beautiful woman, inside out, with such heartwarming gestures, who never made a big deal about them. This woman who knows how to nurture relationships. This fine actor from whom I learnt so much by merely watching and sharing screen space with her, and above all, this wonderful woman who taught me how life should be lived with her laughter and that unmissable glint in the eye, and making the best of life, and whatever it might be offering.

As her dear friend Farooq Shaikh would have said, 'Jeena isi ka naam hai (This is what living life is all about).'

NEERAJ PANDEY

Whenever I met him, his quiet smile just made me feel like all is well with the world and god is in heaven.

He was always an introvert and a quiet person to the world, but he seemed to absorb and observe every word spoken. The amused smile on his face when I blurted out my woes, instantly made me realize, in most cases, the frivolity of something that I had magnified so much in my head.

All that, of course, happened much later, once we became friends.

I met Neeraj Pandey for the first time at the National Film Awards ceremony in Delhi. I was hosting the awards and was in the hotel lobby, waiting for my car to get to the rehearsals. The elevator door opened and I saw two gentlemen walk towards the exit. I instantly recognized one of them as we had worked together in a film which had been quite an adventurous experience for all of us. The film never got completed but I ended up becoming friends with Shital Bhatia. He too is fairly quiet and yet, a very sensitive person. He was always looking out for us during that difficult shoot in the jungles because of the chaos at the shoot.

Once we came back, life, as it is in Mumbai, took over and we gradually lost touch. And here he was, walking towards the exit with another gentleman.

'HEYYYYY SHITAL!' I ran towards him. 'OMG! I'm seeing you after so long! How have you been?'

Both the men looked a bit taken aback by this exuberant show of excitement from a woman who had literally run towards them! It took a few seconds for Shital to register that it was me! Of course, it had to be me, with all my enthusiasm on seeing an old friend. I started chatting with him and asked him a dozen questions. When I did give him a chance to speak, he introduced me to the man standing beside him. 'Meet my friend and partner, Neeraj Pandey,' he said softly.

Equally soft was the hello coming from the gentleman. This time, it was my turn to be a bit taken aback. 'NEERAJ PANDEY! OMG! The one who made *A Wednesday*!?' Both of them had amused smiles on their faces. If I was embarrassing them with my enthusiasm, I don't remember noticing it.

In fact, I followed it up with, 'Hi! I am Divya Dutta!' I extended my hand to introduce myself only to see an amused expression on his face. He didn't say anything but his look made me realize that my introduction had just sounded like the dialogue from the famous scene in *Sholay*: '*Tumhara naam kya hai, Basanti*?' With the continuous chatter I had on with Shital, even a passerby would have understood who I was. His subtle smile seemed to indicate that he knew who I was and he patiently nodded. That somehow brought a smile to my face too, and his quiet wit made me instantly comfortable. Now, I started chatting with him but I couldn't find enough words to tell him how much I had loved *A Wednesday*. I am sure he had heard it many-a-times by then. I goofed up again by saying that the film deserved a National Award! I didn't miss the grin on

Neeraj's face when Shital politely added, 'That's what we are here for. The film has won the National Award and we are going for the rehearsal!'

There was an awkward silence from my side (for a change) and this time, we were all laughing. And that, was the beginning of a beautiful bond.

After getting back to Mumbai, we lost touch. There's something really interesting about Mumbai. We may lose touch but when we meet, more often than not, we pick up from where we left. So, one day (finally!), I got a call from the casting director of Friday Filmworks (Neeraj and Shital's production company) that Neeraj wanted to cast me in his next film and wanted to fix up a meeting in the office. I was, of course, ecstatic! All I had to keep in check was my child-like exuberance (it surfaces only around people I am absolutely at home with) and not mess it up!

I reached the office sharp at 11 a.m. as I was told. The casting director came out to receive me. 'Ma'am, sir will be with you in five minutes.'

I looked around the office and saw posters of *A Wednesday* adorning one of the walls. Some witty and motivational quotes were pinned up on another. I saw everyone engrossed in their work. No unnecessary chit-chat or noise—there was a very disciplined vibe around. I automatically straightened up and reminded myself to keep my chatter in check. The door suddenly opened and Neeraj greeted me with a very bright, 'Madam! How are you?' The tone of his greeting just brightened me up. I instantly felt comfortable again and my straight back eased out a bit on the cushioned chair. Without beating around the bush, he asked me if I'd have tea or coffee. And then, he came straight to the point. 'So, we want you to play Shanti ji in *Special 26*. It's not a very lengthy role. You are repeating one line throughout the film but there's a reason why you have been approached for it and it's a nice one.' It was said as simply as that. As straightforward as it could be and he narrated the gist of it to me. I heard him—spellbound.

Ten minutes into the narration of the plot, I was on the edge of my seat. I was so excited about the plot that I forgot to ask a thousand questions about my role. Strangely, it wasn't bothering me at all to know what exactly I was doing in the film. And it had never happened with me. I'm someone who gets into intricate details of how the role starts; where it goes and, the culmination of the character. But here I was, surprising myself.

Actors can be insecure. We love to know where and how we are placed in the larger scheme of things, but for the first time, I didn't feel the need to ask. Of course, the story was gripping and thrilling but there was something else too that had made me feel so secure—the man who had narrated it. I couldn't place what it was about him. I just knew that I had to do this film.

'Read the script and decide,' he said. Again, for the first time ever, I didn't feel the need to ask for it.

'I am doing it,' I said. 'And I am just coming to have a blast!' I somehow wanted to experience the surprise elements of the story with all its twists and turns. I wanted to act in it not as a 'know-it-all' rehearsed actor but as an 'on-the-edge' student, excited about discovering what to deliver next!

I shook his hand, reminding myself not to look overtly excited. But then, I looked at him again and thought, 'Do I really need to put on layers of formal behaviour in front of this extremely genuine and intelligent man? He would know immediately that I am putting on an act. With someone like him, it's better to just be yourself because he would be the last man to judge you.'

After this conversation with myself, I lowered my guard and felt the comfort of being myself. Then I exclaimed in sheer excitement, 'Yay! I'm finally working with you!' That familiar, quiet smile appeared on his face again and he said, 'Welcome on board, Madam!' I knew he meant it.

My first day of shoot was in Delhi. When I arrived at my given call time, they had already begun shooting some action sequence on the barricaded road. There was lots of hustle and bustle; a row of vanity vans was parked on the side and everyone seemed to be on walkie-talkies, giving or taking instructions. The set was buzzing with activity.

'Wow, you've begun already?' I asked Shital.

'Yes, at 6 a.m. We'll be ready for you in an hour,' he said with a smile.

I must say I was impressed. That was some meticulous planning! But we'll see, I thought to myself. It normally happens that they say it will take an hour, but in shoots, delays in execution or some production issues on set usually end up pushing the shoot time further.

Meanwhile, I wore my Shanti ji costume. When I looked at my reflection in the mirror, I was surprised at this new look as the constable who had just one repetitive dialogue in the entire film. I looked at myself again and wondered, 'Hey, I don't know you at all, Shanti ji. But I'll discover you on the set, my lady. I am sure it's going to be a fun ride!'

And what a fun ride it was!

My first shot was with Jimmy Sheirgill, Anupam Kher and Akshay Kumar. I had to walk through the corridor with them. I exchanged pleasantries in Punjabi with all three. It's a blast on the set when your co-stars are a delight and there's an atmosphere of fun and laughter around. Neeraj joined us and explained the scene. Akshay, Anupam ji, Jimmy and I had to walk through the corridors. While Anupam ji mouthed his lines to Akshay, Jimmy and I were supposed to quietly follow them.

'Silence!' the assistant director shouted and Neeraj said 'Action!'. I could see him walking backwards along with the DoP who held the Steadicam. Neeraj's eyes were completely focused on the small screen on the camera and yet, he kept pace with the speed with which the camera and the DoP were moving backwards. As soon as the shot was cut, a quick set-up of another scene was put in place. Before I knew it, we had finished that entire sequence to be shot there by lunch!

'Break!' the AD announced. Someone came and asked me, 'Sir's asking if you'd like to join everyone for lunch.' 'Of course! I'd love that!'

I went into the vanity van and saw all the foodies together— our DoP Bobby Singh, who's no more now (an absolute fun-loving and jovial guy), was discussing recipes of the dishes laid out in front of us. Neeraj, Shital and Jimmy, all were there. They were all cracking jokes and eating.

'Aaiye, Madam!' Neeraj said.

I sat down and was observing everyone as I ate, acclimatizing myself to the new unit. Then, I watched Neeraj. He was quietly smiling at the jokes being cracked at the table, as if he was there and yet not there.

As I was about to take a second serving, Neeraj got up abruptly and said to Bobby, 'Let's go!'

I wondered why he had left so suddenly. Shital explained patiently, 'Once he's done with his food, he goes to set up the next shot so that it's ready by the time you guys are done with lunch.'

No wasting time. That's why I'd felt he was there and still not there! His mind was actually focused on his next shot. But it never showed in his calm exterior, ever. With him, certain things are always understood. His 'work mode' can motivate you to just cut down your own break time and be on the set, working and enjoying it thoroughly. There is never a dull moment. It is such an adrenaline rush that one never feels tired!

I looked forward to being on the set with him. His instructions were simple and clear—exactly what he needed you to do; he'd join us in between shots for a quick chat and before one realized, he would go back to setting up a shot. It was a roller coaster ride just catching up with the whereabouts of the director. He was everywhere, managing everything perfectly with his inherent ease and smile. I was like a bewildered child wondering what was next. I just loved following instructions and finding Shanti ji in every shot . . . a little more each time as the layers unfolded. What a fabulous journey it was turning out to be!

For an actor, it means a lot when the director trusts you. Neeraj would do that without even making a big deal about it. That enhanced my confidence as an actor a lot more. I also realized that Shanti ji had a lot of driving to do, but not the regular kind of driving. It was driving a jeep at full speed with crazy and sudden turns. The action director had a duplicate ready.

'I want to do it myself, sir,' I said.

The action director wasn't too sure.

Neeraj asked me if I had driven a jeep earlier. 'Arey, I learnt driving on Ma's *khatara* jeep only, so I'd love to do this.'

There was no further discussion. 'Cool, Shanti ji will drive herself.'

I saw a set of pale faces around at this announcement, but there was one man who didn't even look back or discuss it any more.

So, they all gave me a warm-up first to get used to that kind of crazy driving. I began with one set of straight driving shots followed by some twirling the wheel shots and then, I was like a girl in a candy store, loving it and wanting more! What made it more fun was the fact that my director trusted that I could do it. When someone places their unquestioning trust in you, you end up doing better than expected because you want to live up to what you promised.

By then, the paleness on the crew's faces had gone and the unit was excited too. The action director started giving me interesting shots. 'Come very close to the camera and make a sharp turn.' If I was nervous, I didn't show it. The unit stood there with bated breath. It was a long shot, but I was clearly visible, so they couldn't have put a duplicate in any case. One man who looked undeterred was Neeraj and the other who looked amused was Bobby, the DoP.

'Action!' I heard on my walkie-talkie and briskly moved my jeep, at full speed, towards the camera. My heart started pounding and as soon as I came right in front of the camera, I took a sharp U-turn! I heard sighs of relief and sounds of cheers. I felt quite relieved and elated myself. Someone had entrusted me with a tough shot like that. That one man who was still looking unaffected by everything around. By the time I could reach him to say thank you, he had moved to the next location to set up the next shot!

Neeraj has never believed in formalities or putting things into words. With him, it's understood. I am sure he knew he had left behind a woman who was ecstatic about having been trusted to do the tough job.

This was one set I didn't want to leave by the end of the shoot. I had imbibed Shanti ji's character completely. When I looked at myself in the mirror one last time, wearing the *havildar* costume, there was a very satisfying feeling within. 'It's been a pleasure to find you and know you Shanti ji . . .'

I whispered. I had a lump in my throat when I packed up. Where had all the twenty days gone? So much excitement, so much work, so much fun and what an adrenaline rush! I didn't feel like going back to the regular routine back home after this fabulous experience. I had this one man to thank for it all but I knew he would brush it aside.

I won a lot of nominations and awards for Shanti ji. That one line that I repeated throughout the film, 'Asli kaam toh yeh kar rahe hain, hum log toh bas . . .' became a very popular one, one that everyone uses even now that *Special 26* has become another feather in Neeraj Pandey's already busy cap. Normally, when a movie is wrapped up, the cast and crew meet up for a wrap-up party. After that, everyone gets so immersed with their respective work and lives that even if one intends not to, one loses touch until the next assignment.

But I had huge withdrawal symptoms. Normally, I don't really feel like that . . . it felt like I was waiting for the unit to come back. I was waiting to meet Neeraj and Shital like I was waiting to meet my own people and just be. It's so amazing how friendships brew. It's not like we spoke a lot; it's not even like we spent a lot of time together, but something felt amazingly good even in the silence of it all. Where the unspoken is understood, there's really no need to talk. When you feel looked after and cared for, it's a very enriching feeling. I looked forward to going to their office for occasional chai chats. It felt like coming home. There was so much simplicity, so much genuineness, and so much warmth around—no facades, bas lots of apnapan.

Neeraj would, of course, abruptly excuse himself to finish his work and then quickly join Shital and me back. The tradition of the chatter I had started the first time I had met him and his amused look continued. I always blurted out everything that was happening in my life—the highs, of course, but even the

lows. I felt safe sharing my feelings here. Also, whenever I had a
sad story to tell, Neeraj had the same amused expression which
strangely had an amazing impact on me. That expression was
as if trying to tell me, 'Really? You seriously bother about such
small stuff?' It suddenly made my big problem look very small. I
would end up laughing it off, without him even saying a word. I
would go back feeling light and happy, like everything was fine
with the world.

* * *

Seven years had passed and I was starting to get the itch. Neeraj
had made such amazing films during this period and I was in
none! I was missing the adrenaline rush of being on his sets.
He normally always smiled and evaded the question when I
asked him about it. But one fine day, he said, 'When there's
something for you, it will come to you. See all my films and tell
me, was there a role that fit you?' He left me with no answer. He
was right. And then, I let it be, like an obedient person.

Out of the blue, one fine day, I got a call from him! 'Madam!'

I straightened up holding the phone when I heard that
bright voice!

'Yes, sir!' I replied.

'Are you free in September–October?' These words were
like music to my ears.

Wait a minute. Was he offering me something, finally? Yes,
he was!

'I am making *Special Ops*. Would you be free and interested?'

I absorbed what he was saying. It took me a few seconds
before I stopped myself from jumping on my sofa. 'Of course,
I am interested and even if I'm not free, I will make sure I am!'

'Come and meet in office tomorrow then.'

It was déjà vu for me. He narrated the gist of the series and I sat spellbound. He asked if I'd like to go through the script and the scenes and I said no. This time, I wasn't surprising myself. This time, I knew the reason why I didn't feel like asking him anything. I trusted this man completely. As a director and as a human being, both, completely. Plus, I liked being a student on his set—exploring and unfolding the character through his vision.

Neeraj has an earnestness about his craft that you cannot help but revere. He is so sincere about his story that you know he will not compromise on any role—whoever you may be— you will do exactly as much as is required to be done by your character. No more, no less. An actor is chosen for a role with a clear reason—that it adds to his storytelling—so there's no scope for being wasted.

When you know you are in the right hands . . . well . . . you don't really feel the need to ask anything. It's like a child holding a parent's finger and blindly walking where they are led, secure and safe, knowing full well that the parent is going to take them to the correct destination. Actors are like children— we can totally let go of all control once we know we are in the right hands; where the director's vision is crystal clear.

I was back in Delhi with my most favourite team after seven years! I felt that familiar hustle and bustle on the set. There is constant activity on the set when Neeraj is around! Not a dull moment. Like in the earlier instance, twenty days went by in a jiffy! Every day was fabulous. Something new, something exciting, always. . .

I was discovering my character, Sadia, from Neeraj's perspective again and midway, I realized what I was actually doing. What magical moments I was a part of! I was absorbing and cherishing each moment! Behind that quietude was a supremely intelligent man who got his audience on the edge of their seat with the sheer thrill he provided in his films. For the first time, I felt like the audience while enacting a part. There was a surge of excitement about what was going to happen next in that absolutely thrilling shoot.

In a heartbeat, those days, which were full of shoots and fun group dinners, were over and I was sad about leaving, once again. But this time, it wasn't a long wait since I got a call from Neeraj again during the last leg of the lockdown. They were making a short film on domestic violence and Phalguni, the talented costume designer who was part of all Neeraj Pandey movies, was going to direct it. We all met on a group video call and he heard us rehearse—as always, he didn't say anything but absorbed everything and wished us good luck.

In six months, I'd done two amazing projects with him. He had kept his word. 'When there's something for you, it will come to you . . .' I wanted to thank him again but when does he ever feel comfortable with these formalities? So, I called him and said my consistently most favourite line, 'Can I come and see you?'

'Yes, come tomorrow.'

We chatted. Again, I vented out a few woes. His smile, again, made me feel how silly and irrelevant they were. Then, he abruptly got up to write an email and joined Shital and me back again. As I was about to leave, he said, 'No, wait.'

A few unit members in office brought in a cake to celebrate my birthday. I was overwhelmed. In a big city like Mumbai where everyone is so engrossed in their own lives and *bhag-daud* (running around), there are a few, who, in their subtle, quiet ways, understand you and care for you and are always there—that is my big reward and a huge blessing.

Neeraj, Shital and Friday Filmworks, for me, are my home ground. My go-to people.

As Neeraj accompanied me to the elevator to see me off, there were a thousand things I wanted to say. I had always chatted away, while he listened quietly with that smile of his. However, this time, I was quiet too. Sometimes, you should just let silence do the talking.

Even though I didn't say it then, I do want to say it now. Thank you, Neeraj, for being you, for your amazing films, for making me a part of a few of them, for this friendship, for this bond, for that smile which takes away all my silly worries.

With people like you around, everything is surely fine with the world. And yes, god is in heaven.

DHARMENDRA

**He had always been close to my heart. After all, he was *mere*
Punjab *da puttar*! And more so because we belong to the
same town in Punjab, Sahnewal. My mother was posted as a
civil surgeon in Sahnewal.**

During my childhood, I would hear someone or the other
coming to visit Ma for a consultation say, '*Dharam ji aye the
raat ko apna ghar, gulliyan sab dekha . . .*' They would say that
he sat in the nooks and corners that were reminiscent of his
younger days, got extremely emotional and left the same night.

When I overheard these conversations, the little me thought,
'Arey, why didn't he go visit his house during the daytime? Why
did he leave quietly overnight? I wish I could see him! I wish I
could talk to him! My *Sholay* star!'

I was so proud that I belonged to the same town as him! I
would always hear that many people from Sahnewal used to go
visit Dharam ji in Mumbai (Bombay then) and were warmly
welcomed in his household.

My uncle, Deepak Bahry, who was also a renowned
filmmaker at that time, was making a film with Dharam ji
and we were visiting my uncle in Bombay during our summer

holidays. My Nana (maternal grandfather) took Ma and me to meet Dharam ji's father, who was fondly called Master ji as he used to be a teacher in Sahnewal, at their huge bungalow in the plush Juhu area.

We met Master ji, a gracious man who spoke in staunch Punjabi, with my Nana and Ma. They were discussing the good old days and chatting away. Amidst all this, the graceful Prakash ji walked in, carrying Punjab *ke* famous *aatewale* biscuits and masala chai for us. More conversation in Punjabi ensued. It didn't feel like Bombay at all! It felt like a warm affectionate Punjabi household back home. I was listening to them and also looking around, hoping to catch a glimpse of Dharam ji. But we were told later that he was shooting. I was a bit disappointed. I really wanted to see him. Well, maybe another time, I consoled myself. I came back home to Punjab and bragged at school about my visit to Dharmendra's house. Somewhere in my heart, I was hoping to be an actor too . . . wishing to be in Mumbai!

Years later, when I became an actor and was signed up to do a film called *Apne* starring all the three Deols, it was a kind of homecoming for me. All three sons of Punjab and me, the daughter. I was very emotional about it. Back home, it would mean a lot to all the people to see the four of us together as a family in a film.

I first met Dharam ji on the sets of *Apne*. I confidently went up to him and introduced myself in Punjabi. He was delighted! '*Deepak di paanji hain na?* (You are Deepak's niece?)'

I nodded.

He made me sit next to him and we started chatting as if we had known each other for a very long time. He asked me about Ma and about our town, Sahnewal.

'Is that hospital still there?' And I nodded in sheer enthusiasm, super excited about sharing fond memories of the same place with him. After a bit, he said, 'I know you wanted to be an actor and also that your uncle was sceptical about it. Honestly, even I was. But I am glad you are in this film, playing my daughter.' I managed a smile, absorbing his straight-from-the-heart talk.

My first shot with him shall always be very special. I kept looking at his handsome face and absorbing the fact that I was acting with the man I had been wanting to meet since childhood . . . a man who I had been hearing about from everyone I had known since childhood.

He warmly patted my back after the shot and said, '*Aaja, cha peeyengi*? (Will you have tea?)'

Of course! He then asked me curiously what my dream role would have been. Before I could reply, he added, 'Actually I would love to see you in a role like *Guddi*!' And I added, 'Then would you play yourself again in it as you are my favourite star too?' Both of us laughed and as we did, I kept admiring his infectious laughter and his warmth for me.

Apne went on to become a big blockbuster and the film fulfilled one big dream for me. When I went back home, everyone in Punjab said, 'We feel so proud to see you work with Dharam ji, Sunny and Bobby together. All our people in the same frame is a treat for us!'

From then on, I became the official *Punjab di kudi*.

Many years later, Ma, my brother Rahul and I flew to Canada for a Punjabi awards evening that I was going to host. Many stalwarts from Punjab, including Dharam ji and Prem Chopra ji, were there too. It was Raksha Bandhan just a day before the awards. Ma said, 'Listen, I want to meet Dharam ji.'

A message was sent to his suite and we were instantly invited. My mother was not so big on rituals so she just carried the *rakhi* and *mithai* in her hand. But what I saw later was heartwarming. I saw a very emotional Dharam ji getting the rakhi tied from Ma and an equally sentimental Nalini (Ma) hugging him! And all this while I was standing in a corner, getting teary-eyed at seeing this brother-sister duo's affection, in a typical Punjabi way.

I knew Dharam ji was extremely fond of poetry and so was Ma, so she had taken along her book of poems as a gift for her brother. '*Main zaroor padunga*,' he promised my misty-eyed mother. That day, a new bond with my hero was formed, thanks to my mother.

Dharam ji was to be awarded the lifetime achievement award at that event.

Apart from hosting the event, I had also put together a performance based on a medley of all his popular numbers as a tribute. It was a high to perform on his songs while he sat there cheering me . . . this man with the most endearing smile ever! After the performance, I announced his lifetime achievement award and felt so proud. His journey from Punjab to Mumbai had been amazing. He was easily the most handsome among the heroes we've had and the distinct variety of roles he's played is truly tremendous. I think he's excelled in every genre, action being the primary one, of course. His patent dialogue, '*Kutte, main tera khoon pi jaaonga* . . .' became crazy popular but he was a natural with romance too. His eyes and smile could sweep any woman off her feet as he sang, '*Pal pal dil ke paas* . . .' My personal favourite though are his comedies. Who could play Professor Parimal Tripathi aka Pyare Mohan better than him in *Chupke Chupke*? That's a film I have seen at least thirty-five times, never getting enough of Pyare Mohan's antics in his extremely charming style!

The handsome star walked up the stage to take his award. His speech was very emotional and straight from the heart.

After a huge standing ovation, as he was walking back from the stage, I started to make my next announcement. I suddenly heard murmurs and laughter. Before I could realize what had happened, a pair of arms hugged me from behind. As I turned, I saw a smiling Dharam ji!

I was in for a pleasant surprise when he took the mic, pointed towards me and announced, 'I am very proud of this *baccha* of mine.' Holding me, he said emotionally, '... when she joined the movies, I wasn't too keen, but I am glad she didn't listen to me. She makes me proud, very proud!' He then kissed my forehead affectionately.

There was a loud cheer from the audience. He gave me back the mic and walked towards his seat. I stood there dumbfounded. What a gracious man! What a generous statement! How many people would pour their heart out in public so honestly? To say that he was sceptical wasn't easy but he said it in all honesty in front of a large audience. More importantly, he felt the need to say it. I could see my mother in the audience. And yes, she was crying. Her brother had just given her daughter his approval in public and she was proud and elated.

My respect for him increased manifold that day and so did my confidence in myself!

Unfortunately, after that, I didn't get the chance to meet him. But I did go to Sahnewal when I was shooting in Chandigarh as I wanted to visit the place that had been home in my childhood, the place that held the fondest memories of my parents and my childhood.

I covered my face and walked the corridors of Ma's hospital. I could still hear her voice ordering the nurse to get her stuff and telling the driver to get the jeep. The hustle and bustle that used to surround her echoed in my head. Tears were trickling down my face as I went past her office.

Suddenly, someone called out, 'Divya ji?' It was a staff nurse. I replied with a quick 'Ji' and *'Sat Sri Akal ji'* and left. I wanted this walk down memory lane to be my solo journey . . . just me and my memories. I went to the old *gullys*, to the old house, everywhere and then, I sat alone, reminiscing.

After all these years, I had got the answer to why Dharam ji went alone to all those places and left before anyone could realize. Yes, I had learnt it the practical way.

The next day, the newspapers there reported: 'Divya Dutta revisits her hometown quietly and leaves in the morning'.

This was exactly what the emotional Dharam ji had been doing all these years—reliving his connect with his early days, with his Punjab *ki mitti*.

In a very strange way, that day in Sahnewal, I stood connected with the feelings of this one man of the soil, Dharmendra.

I had a strong urge to speak to him, so I called him up to hear his warm voice. 'I really want to see you, sir,' I said.

He was in Khandala, at his farm, where he has been spending most of his time these days. *'Main wapas aana haan taan zaroor milde haan. Bade saal ho gaye* (Let's meet when I am back. It's been ages),' he said.

Yes, it has been years. I can't wait to see you; can't wait to chat with you; can't wait to discuss poetry with you, and someday . . . work with you again.

And I can't wait to hear that shy laughter and those words, 'Cha peeyengi?'

NITIN KAKKAR

Everyone was raving about this small but extremely soulful and hilarious film after its preview was held at a theatre in suburban Mumbai. This film—*Filmistaan*—later went on to win the National Award. I met the director of that film, Nitin Kakkar, for the first time at that very preview only. He was quiet, reserved, polite, and spoke only when spoken to.

I enthusiastically went up to congratulate him for a fabulous first film. He seemed pretty uneasy with compliments but managed a smile. And I found it very sweet. We exchanged numbers, and promised to meet over coffee, which we soon did.

That day, I broke the ice by chatting nineteen to the dozen. He initially just heard me out but soon, with great gusto, joined in the conversation, which then went on for the longest time. Yes, we got along well. He promised to narrate his next film, *Ram Singh Charlie,* to me. I went to hear it at his office, a few days later.

This man was a revelation to me! The way he narrated the film, I sat spellbound. He seemed so engrossed in the world of his characters that he became one with them while telling their story. There was a lump in my throat when he finished. One, because of the story itself and two, due to the sheer passion with which this young man was narrating his story.

That's how one should feel for their craft. And yes, that strongly.

I could feel his world. I could feel the passion he had to make this film, and he was putting in all his money along with two of his friends (the super talented actors Sharib Hashmi and Umesh Pawar). He wanted to make this film his way, with no obstruction in his vision from any outside diktats.

I was quiet (for a change). I was distinctly impressed with Nitin and his storytelling. The film was about how a simple man who plays the clown in a circus, along with his wife Kajri and their son, goes out to the bigger circus of life when the circus he works for shuts down. He's torn between making a living and following his passion.

I came back home but could not get the film out of my head. The very next morning, I called Nitin. 'Good morning, I want to do this film. I want to play the wife.'

He replied, 'Oh okay, come to the office and we will chat.'

Over a cup of tea, which he always likes to make himself, we sat quietly. He was immersed in his thoughts and said, 'You know, Divya, it will be my absolute pleasure to work with you, but it's a small film with real characters and you are a glamorous face. You won't fit in.'

I was taken aback and retorted, 'Listen, but I have done Shyam Benegal and Rituparno Ghosh movies. That's as real as it can get, so why not this then?'

He said, 'You are an established face. Putting you in the film with the rest of the cast might look out of place.'

This time, the hunger to do a film that would surely be a very cherished experience and the challenge of being perceived differently by this talented director sitting in front of me, finally made me say something quite bluntly. 'So, you are the director of the film. If you believe I can do this role, then you change this glamorous face perception, na—both for yourself and the audiences. Give me a look and attitude that is very different from what I have been seen in so far. On my part, I promise to learn and follow what you say. There's nothing better than a hungry actor.'

I couldn't believe I had said that but it seemed to have impacted him and well, me too!

'Okay, give me some time,' he said as he came to see me off.

I added, 'Actually, meet some other actors too, and if you come back to me, I promise I'll live up to what you want Kajri to be.'

After about two weeks, I heard from him. 'Come to the office.'

Workshops were being held for the film with Kumud Mishra (another super talented actor who was to play the titular role) and a few theatre actors. Nitin took me to his cabin. 'Okay, so I really thought about it. I also met a few other actors, but I think I'll go with you.'

There was a twinkle in my eye. I couldn't wait to experience how this person, who narrated a film like a dream, would direct it!

I said happily, 'As promised, I am ready to learn.'

He added calmly, 'I want you to unlearn.'

What did he mean by that, I wondered?

He continued, 'I want you to drop all your learnings as an experienced actor and become a clean slate. Absolutely raw. Like a newcomer. To become Kajri.'

I kept gaping at him. 'How would I do that?'

He explained, 'You have mastered the art of acting. I need you to drop your perfections.'

It was then that I understood the meaning of what he had said. 'Wow! You just made it super tough but I love it, I'll take it on!' I said beaming.

In that moment I knew I was getting into something I had never done before and I was all set to rediscover myself as an actor—and to 'unlearn!'

I too attended workshops for the film. Before that, I hadn't ever done so many workshops for any film. The best part was that I hardly had any dialogues to rehearse for. My only job was to come and sit in the workshop, and interact with my co-stars . . . bas. I wondered what I was doing there but I was doing what I had promised.

The tough part came during the look test. I had already been told that it was a no make-up look. Now no make-up look in filmi terms is considered to be 'minimal make-up', like I used to do in Shyam Benegal films, just a light base and *kajal*. So, I did the same. Nitin looked at me and said, 'Don't cheat, remove that make-up. No make-up at all!'

I was devastated. 'But my dark circles might show.' I literally pleaded.

He calmly answered, 'I want to see the dark circles. I want to see the real you.'

I had now begun to understand the true meaning of unlearning, step by step. I was so used to at least that bare minimum make-up. As actors, we are so vain. We need to look good all the time (because we are being watched all the time) but I had no choice here. I went to the washroom, and reluctantly washed my face. I was so conscious of coming out like that in front of people. I opened the door and nervously went in front of Nitin again. I did feel exposed, showing the 'real me' to all the crew standing there with him.

He looked at me and said, 'Yes, I love this.' I surely didn't.

We went to Kolkata for the shoot and I was super nervous and excited. For my first shot, I took ages to come out. Not that I was doing any make-up, but I was giving myself a pep

With Mr Bachchan who launched *Me and Ma*,
and made it truly memorable!

With Mr Bachchan at his annual Diwali bash
at his residence. Selfie time!

That big warm hug from Dharam ji at an awards event where he said, 'Proud of you, bachche!' Life came full circle with these words.

Ma tying a rakhi on Dharam ji's wrist, cementing a bond for life. A priceless moment.

With Gulzar saab when I met him officially for the first time to discuss our chat session and it felt as if I had known him for ever.

With Gurdas Maan at a photoshoot. Looking suave and endearing as always.

Warmth personified, with Gurdas Maan and his wife, Manjeet Maan, at their house.

A happy moment with my super talented co-star Irrfan Khan in the vanity van during one of our shoots.

With Javed saab at his residence. Always smiling in his company.

With Javed saab and Farhan, two of my favourite men! At a get-together at Javed saab and Shabana ji's house.

Another candid moment with Shabana ji and Javed saab at their place.

All smiles with Juhi Chawla in a shikara in Kashmir. Enjoying kahwa during the shoot of *Sukhmani*.

Juhi and Sonali at the launch of *Me and Ma*, where the two lovely ladies read an excerpt each.

With my Santa, Rajit Kapur, at one of our favourite hang-outs.

It started during *Train to Pakistan*—friends for life. With Rajit Kapur and Richa Gupta Kala (who was an associate director on the film).

Showing me a new path. Being directed by Rakeysh
Omprakash Mehra during the filming of *Delhi-6*.

After the most iconic scene in *Bhaag Milkha Bhaag*, with
Rakeysh Omprakash Mehra and Farhan Akhtar.

One of the most fun and adorable co-actors to work
with: Farhan Akhtar.

Etched in my mind: this was my last meeting with Rishi Kapoor at the Prithvi Theatre where he was so happy and full of life.

Starry-eyed: my first-ever meeting with Salman when I hadn't even joined the movies. At the launch of my uncle Deepak Bahry's film.

This photograph is special as it was clicked by Salman himself on the sets after a shoot.

Happiest with her, at the rehearsals for *Sheer Qorma*.

With the two enigmatic ladies, Shaukat Azmi and Shabana Azmi.

Our favourite *adaab* pose at one of Shabana ji's get-togethers. Hope I've got it right by now!

A selfie with Shyam babu (Shyam Benegal) during one of our chai sessions at his office.

All attentive to the instructions, loving being directed by Shyam babu on the sets of *Bose*. Also in the picture are Sachin Khedekar and Jisshu Sengupta.

A meeting with *dost* Sonali at her home after she
returned from New York.

With my bestie Sonu at his place.

With the charming
Shah Rukh Khan
at Javed saab's
birthday party.

With Nitin Kakkar and Sharib
Hashmi (actor and co-producer)
having our fun time post the
screening of *Ram Singh Charlie*
as the opening film at IFFI,
Goa, in 2015.

Finding my shanti (pun intended)!
On the sets of *Special 26* with
Neeraj Pandey.

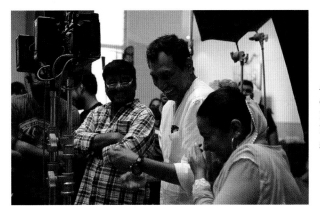

All laughs and a lot of work. With Neeraj Pandey and Shivam Nair (director) on the sets of *Special Ops*.

Acing the nuances under the superb direction of Sriram Raghavan. With him and Varun Dhawan on the sets of *Badlapur*.

With the camera-shy Sriram Raghavan on my birthday.

With my very own Jaggu dada
(Jackie Shroff).

'All is well' wali feeling. With
Raju Hirani, Vicky Kaushal,
Boman Irani and Kanika
Dhillon at Raju Hirani's
Diwali party.

With Naseer saab at a
get-together at Janki Kutir.

Selfie with Anupam Kher.

With Anupam Kher and his mother Dulari aunty at a screening.

With Anubhav Sinha at the red carpet event of his movie screening.

With Prem Chopra and his wife Uma ji at the wedding of
my brother, Rahul, and to-be sister-in-law, Shweta.

With my uncle Deepak Bahry at my place.

talk to go in front of the camera sans make-up for the first time ever . . . like I used to be in school or college. Yes, I did feel like a raw newcomer.

The biggest challenge came my way after a while. We were all set to shoot an emotional scene when Nitin came up to me and whispered, 'So listen, I know you excel in your emotional scenes and are known for them. Just a request, I don't want you to shed any tears!'

I stumbled hearing that one. 'But this is a very emotional scene, *rona aa gaya toh?* (What if tears start falling?)' I thought he was being hard now.

'*Toh rok lena* (then stop them). No tears! That's the unlearning too.'

I stood there, full of nervousness for my first shot, without make-up and an instruction about not shedding a single tear! Then what was I supposed to do? I think I said it out aloud, and he answered, 'That is what you have to discover!'

That day, I actually felt like a rank newcomer, not sure of anything I was going to do. But there was one thing I was clear about—I had to please this hard-to-please director!

He explained the shot beautifully to me: It was with my husband, who comes to pick me up in his hand-pulled rickshaw. Nitin told me their backstory; their dynamics as a couple, and then said, 'Now, flow!'

And then the magic happened.

Without all that make-up, and in that costume, I felt I was Kajri. Divya was nowhere!

With all the workshops where I sat mutely watching Kumud speak his lines, my comfort level with him had gone up so much that I felt I knew him as Ram Singh inside out, and my expressions and reactions to him came out effortlessly.

I did feel an urge to cry but I refrained from doing so. The unshed tears were held in check by an expression that I myself hadn't expected.

While doing that shot, I could feel that I wasn't acting. I was feeling Kajri. Nitin had subtly but surely removed Divya completely from within me and let Kajri sink in, without me even realizing the magic that he had woven around me.

In a few days, I had become extremely comfortable coming to shoot with my dark circles, eager and curious to know what Kajri would make me do next!

This experience, of shooting with Nitin Kakkar, is by far the most distinct one for me. I loved each moment of being nervous, of unlearning and rediscovering myself, thanks to him.

On the last day of the shoot, I was pretty sad. Nitin came and in his usual, quiet way, whispered, 'I am really happy. You really brought Kajri alive.'

I got emotional. 'Thank you for this new Divya, *naye pack mein*.' I tried laughing but I was sad. I was going to miss this set. I was going to miss being directed by Nitin.

When we saw the film, I was amazed and choked yet again. Nitin had poured his heart and soul into making this beautiful film and I was so proud. And who was this new actor cast as Kajri? I smiled. I loved how my scenes had turned out (yes, without tears) and I told Ma who was sitting next to me, '*Ma, main toh sundar lag rahi hun yaar!* (I'm looking pretty!)' I had finally learnt to love being in my own skin and share it with the world.

I came out of the preview theatre and hugged Nitin tightly (never mind his shy disposition). For this beautiful experience I cherish as an actor, *ek hug to banti thi* (one hug was required).

After that, we became very good friends. Nitin actually managed to talk a lot with me gradually. I always went to him for advice. I remember landing at his office once, all confused. I had been offered a very good film with a very good role but it was supposed be a very bold one too.

'You are a super actor; you will kill it. Don't doubt yourself. You are an actor. Sink your teeth in it and have a blast.' His words gave me the confidence that I sometimes forget I possess. I said yes to that film and went on to get many awards for it.

I'm glad I listened to Nitin but haven't I always, my ever-dependable director dost?

Chalo, I am coming to office soon to ask for another beautiful role. To unlearn again and find myself again—naye pack mein!

IRRFAN KHAN

I was on the set of a film called *Dubai Return*. It was a crazy, whacky comedy, and I was told it had a super talented cast, led by Irrfan Khan.

I was most excited about meeting the brilliant actor on the set. I was playing a Lolita kind of role to a gangster (played by Vijay Maurya) who later gets married to her. The story was about a defamed gangster, played by Irrfan, who comes back to Mumbai to clear his name and prove his mettle with the help of his friends. He ends up failing, in a hilarious twist of events.

The first day of shoot with Irrfan was for a very funny scene—Irrfan had to pester me to enter his friend's house and I (playing the friend's wife) had to throw him out and then scold him and send him away, but not before he had troubled me enough. It was a very humorous scene, and we were cracking up just reading it. I realized that both Irrfan and I were not too much into rehearsing. We both believed in the magic of the actual shot (but that was later, after *Dubai Return*, when we did a few more films together). For this one, I wasn't prepared for what was in store for me that day.

I was playing a Marathi woman. Since I was new to Mumbai, I was still learning Marathi. So, I had mugged up the few words

I was supposed to mouth and was supposedly all set to face my crazily talented co-star, who seemed to be totally chilling in a corner. Then, we were called on set and introduced to each other.

The first thing I noticed about him was his shy smile, the one that reached his eyes, those magical eyes. He said 'Hi', with that warm smile, and we went to rehearse. We both did our lines once. He was observing me, and I noticed that, but he didn't say anything or offer any suggestions or advice, despite being a senior actor.

The scene required me to snatch a glass that he had picked from my house and push him out of the house. So, both of us did a rehearsal to get an idea of our movements and activity. I snatched the glass from him in the rehearsal, and then we were all set to shoot. As the director said, 'Action,' I started mouthing my lines, and tried to snatch the glass from him. I think I did notice that naughty glint in Irrfan's eyes as he decided to improvise. I tried snatching it again but he wouldn't leave the glass. I was a bit surprised, but played along. Whatever little Marathi I knew, I rattled off, shouting at him to get out of the house but return my precious glass before that.

He suddenly dropped the glass from his hand and it broke into pieces. He added, '*Le tera glass* (Take your glass),' literally teasing me. Now this I wasn't prepared for, but wanted to keep going. My shocked expression as to what had just happened helped me pick up from where Irrfan had left his improvisation. I shrieked loudly, and pushed him, yelling, 'Get out!' I said it a few times and mixed it with some lines of my own, while physically pushing him out, much more aggressively and in a far more animated fashion than I was supposed to. And the end result was that it looked crazy funny, or so everyone on the set thought. I heard a loud cheer as the director yelled out 'Cut!' Then he came up to me excitedly and said, 'Wow, I love what you both did to the scene, way better than what was written. Awesome chemistry!'

Irrfan said thank you shyly, and went back to his corner. This time, I pulled up a chair and sat with him. 'This was so much fun! I wasn't ready for that impromptu stuff, but it was so much fun and it turned out so well,' I uttered, all excited.

'*Tum accha improvise karti ho. Iska mazaa hi alag hai. Sahi sur pakda tumne* (You improvise very well. It's much more interesting. You caught on brilliantly),' he said softly with that same smile.

From then on, I understood the magic of the moment. There are some things an actor needs to know beforehand, but some, one must leave to the magic of the moment. All you need to do is be alert and stay willing to respond to the newness of it. I started enjoying that very much. I used to look forward to what Irrfan would throw my way, to catch it and respond with equal fervour.

The whole unit would gather to see when Irrfan was in a shot. There was a curiosity and intrigue to his performance that everyone loved—the unexpected was expected, everyone waited with bated breath to see him take the scene a few notches higher, always, while he performed. That was the magic of one of the finest actors we ever had, Irrfan Khan.

Sadly, that film didn't get released, but the who's who of the industry had seen its previews and had called it a cult film. Well, that was that. With the film and with Irrfan. Until I met him again for Yash Raj's *Aaja Nachle*.

I remember being called for a narration with Aditya Chopra. It was Madhuri Dixit's comeback film, and everyone was very excited. I loved the script and my role, and of course, since it was my second film with the Yash Raj banner after *Veer-Zaara*, I was very comfortable about being presented well.

The only thing I was curious to know was who was going to play my husband. 'Well, I wanted it to be a surprise,' he said. But when he saw the expression on my face, he decided to share the news. 'Don't want to say it too soon, but it might be Irrfan. Talks are on.' If I was super excited to share screen space with Irrfan, I tried not to show it. How wonderful would it be to weave magic with him again and also to improvise those beautifully nuanced scenes written for us.

This time, when we met on the sets, it was more like friends, the familiar comfort of having worked together. One thing remained unchanged. His shy smile.

We exchanged pleasantries, and our lines; our relationship angle in the film this time was romantic, subtle and nuanced. And yes, this time around too, we didn't really rehearse—just said the lines together once.

I had fewer lines. It was a scene where Irrfan was to gift me a necklace and ask me for a favour, a very interesting scene. I was wondering how to react to each of his lines, how to sit so that it would be comfortable for him to put the necklace around my neck, etc. Too many thoughts, too many questions swirled in the head. But Irrfan looked as calm as always. I didn't see him memorize his lines either, or look tense or apprehensive. I was wondering how the scene would go. Amidst all my thoughts, I heard the director say, 'Action!'

Irrfan came and sat next to me. I saw a different person, suddenly. He came and delivered his lines, and soon, I was so absorbed in just listening to him (I had my back towards him, so it was only his voice reaching me). That voice expressing a zillion emotions in one line, that voice modulating in several different ways, and above all, that voice which came straight from the heart. Then, I turned to look at him in the scene. Just looking into those eyes—full of sincerity, genuineness, and love—was so mesmerizing that for those few seconds, I forgot that I was Divya and he was Irrfan.

He transported me into the world of that couple, of Farookh and Najma. He effortlessly put the necklace around my neck, and then there was silence from his side. *Had he forgotten his dialogues?* It would be blasphemous to even think that. He was looking into my eyes. What the dialogues left unsaid was conveyed by his eyes. I forgot we were even acting and just reacted to that silence, to those eyes, to that shy smile.

As an actor, I felt something amazing had been accomplished in that scene that day. That was Irrfan! Absolute magic. All I had to do this time too was only react to the magic he was weaving, and it rubbed off on me too. He had made it that easy. *Isn't acting about reactions?* And if the actor is of the prowess of Irrfan, it just can't get any better.

Working with Irrfan was addictive. You can't settle for anything less in scenes, that brilliance is unparalleled. Those silences are magical, that chemistry, unquestionable. All that coming from a man I'd barely spoken to in my real life, except pleasantries. Unbelievable!

That was that again, with Irrfan.

I kept watching the brilliant work he was doing and the newer heights he was scaling, from Indian to international films, and becoming a name to reckon with in Hollywood. I kept wondering when I would get to work with him again. One fine day, my manager called and informed me that renowned filmmaker David Lynch's daughter, Jennifer Lynch, was making a film called *Hisss*, with Mallika Sherawat playing a *naagin*. And Irrfan was in the lead role. I had been offered the other lead role of his wife in it. I jumped with sheer joy as I hung up and broke into bhangra mode at home. Everyone was wondering what had happened to me. I danced my way to mom, and broke the news in a sing-song way, 'Yayyy! I'm working with Irrfan again! Yippie! Party time!' Yes, party time as an actor, an absolute treat.

We flew together to Kerala, where the shoot was happening. Finally, in so many years, Irrfan actually spoke to me, about how he began his career, his experiences and his friends. It was so refreshing to have a normal conversation, nothing related to films, just about the life of a simple man who came to Mumbai with dreams and a passion to realize them, and made it against all odds and how! It was so amazing to know that he remembered every minute detail about the people he met, the work he did, the struggles and the opportunities.

He also recollected where he had met me for the first time, way before we shot together. I had visited the sets of *Banegi Apni Baat*, and he reminisced fondly about his first impression of the simple girl from a small town, in all her innocence. I was truly amazed. There was so much to talk to him about! What an interesting man with a crazy, witty side to him. He cracked subtle jokes with a straight face. I had to quickly grab on to them before I missed them and when I did, I laughed out loud at the hilarity of the anecdotes he was narrating. It had been a fun chat. A big change from what I was used to with Irrfan earlier, just basic pleasantries. I didn't even realize when we landed in picturesque Kerala.

Jennifer proved to be a very passionate director—soft, full of life, and yet so immersed in her film. We loved working with her. She would pamper her actors silly and get them to deliver what she wanted with so much sensitivity. Irrfan was in the role of the investigating cop, and was, as expected, very calm and chilled out.

Except for one day.

We were told that there was an intimate scene between the couple. I was a bit nervous on set, but Jennifer was trying to infuse confidence in me by telling me the backstory of the couple to get me into the mood. It made me feel a bit lighter but I was unsure how I'd do an intimate scene with someone who I so looked up to. There was too much pressure to not mess it up or show my nervousness. To add to it all, I knew Irrfan would be his usual cool and composed self. But I was mistaken.

All the assistants were looking for Irrfan, but he was nowhere to be seen, until someone saw him on the terrace of the house we were shooting in, alone.

Jennifer quickly went to him. I saw both of them in a deep, quiet conversation. Actually, I could only see Jennifer talking, and Irrfan was just listening, looking far, far away. I was very curious to know what it was all about, and join them, but I refrained. To my surprise, Jennifer called out to me, 'Divya, join us please!' I did.

'So . . .' she said. There was a long pause before she spoke again, and Irrfan was still quiet. 'Irrfan's a bit nervous!' I couldn't believe what I'd heard and looked at Irrfan, who looked so child-like and tense. I had never seen him like that.

I strangely felt very protective towards him, and broke into laughter. 'That makes two of us! I am a bit nervous too!' Jennifer smiled, but Irrfan was still quiet. Strangely, I felt a little in control of the situation, and took over, for a change.

I went and sat with Irrfan on the terrace parapet, and we had a cup of chai together. I chatted and this time, he only listened to me, he didn't talk. He was somewhere else . . . till I cracked a joke and that was that. I could finally see that shy smile again! Jennifer held our hands and we were back on the set. 'We will just do one shot, so give it all your magic,' she said.

Everyone was quiet on set. It was an emotional scene too, along with being intimate; a beautiful moment between a husband and a wife. Jennifer said a very soft, 'Action', and then the magic happened. The lines poured out from Irrfan like a stream of beautiful music. A soft whisper, full of emotions. A husband pouring out his heart to his wife. I could feel the tears trickling from the corner of my eye as he held me close. It's a woman's instinct when a man holds her. I was immediately comfortable, in fact, felt protected and taken care of.

The man who was tense and nervous only a while ago had taken charge as an actor now. He made sure I was comfortable, and not awkward about anything, and I wasn't. There was an unspoken bond I shared with him in that moment, and I knew I didn't have to be nervous at all. This actor-par-excellence was now looking over everything.

We could hear applause when we finished. The crew was clapping. I saw tears of joy in Jennifer's eyes as she came to hug the two of us. 'Thank you, for the most beautiful scene ever!' Irrfan looked relaxed now, a glint in his eyes. I'm sure he was not too comfortable doing that scene, but he had taken charge as an actor and risen above his own apprehensions and made sure I was at ease too.

As is always the case with him, *makhan ki tarah smooth scene hua* (it went off as smoothly as butter). I chirpily went up to Irrfan again, pulled a chair and said, 'So, I want to say thank you. You made it so easy and comfortable.'

I had seen another side of him that day, the caring, soft side, of making sure that the co-actor was in good spirits. That day, I found a friend in him. *Hisss* was a beautiful experience for me personally—a beautiful role, a fabulous director and, the best co-actor I could ask for. I came back home very happy, a satiated actor.

Well, that was that again, with the elusive Irrfan. From then on, I would send him a message once in a while, and we'd bump into each other at occasions, but we never really got to sit and chat one-on-one. I invited him over once for my birthday; crew members from some of my recent films, friends and colleagues were coming too. The entire gang of *Welcome to Sajjanpur* including Shyam Benegal and his wife Nira, to the friends I made while filming *Hisss*. I never thought Irrfan would actually come. On request, Sonu Nigam was singing a song for us, and everyone was dancing and making merry. And the doorbell rang. A face peeped in from the dimly-lit lobby. I was ecstatic.

He did show up, though a bit awkward in the crowd. He handed me a bouquet of flowers, had a piece of cake, sat for some time and then left, but not before narrating an interesting anecdote to everyone and bringing a big smile on their faces. '*Milte hain* (We'll meet),' he said. Yes, that was that.

On another occasion, I was shooting for yet another film with some young stars, and they were discussing the best actors we had. Obviously, the topic shifted to Irrfan, and how the young actor had really prepared himself to face 'the Irrfan Khan' in a scene. He had worked out his dialogues, mannerisms, look and everything. He had planned each mannerism and expression so well, but '. . . the moment Irrfan sir came, he just did it with so much ease and effortlessness that I just left all that I had thought I would do and only reacted!' He beamed, laughing at himself.

That did sound familiar, minus the over-preparedness part. I felt a surge of pride, for having known Irrfan and having worked with him. I just smiled when anyone mentioned Irrfan with such reverence!

We kept bumping on flights and events. He was in and out of the country, and I was eagerly waiting again to be on set with him.

It happened with Abhinay Deo's *Blackmail*. Unfortunately, I didn't have any scenes with Irrfan in the film, but we were called together for a workshop. Well, I was delighted to see him after so long; his sense of humour on full display, and we were all laughing. We read one scene and Irrfan told Abhinay, '*Yaar, prawns khilao badhiya se.*'

The food was ordered and the workshop had now become a session on food, where everything from recipes to favourite dishes were discussed, and by the time the food arrived, everyone literally pounced on it. After that lunch, he said, '*Set pe karte hain baaki.*' He flashed his charismatic smile. Everyone agreed happily.

I never met him on the set of that film. I could do so only after the film was complete when we were promoting it. I met him at Mehboob Studios. He was leaving and I had just arrived. I sent a message that I wanted to meet him before he left. I quickly went to his vanity van. His staff was packing his stuff. I gifted him my book and chatted. When one is in a hurry, how much can they talk? It was just very nice to see him. He cracked a subtle joke, and yes, I grabbed it before I missed.

We both laughed. '*Bhagta hun, milte hain* (I've got to run, we will meet again),' he said. This time that was really that. I never met him again. I never saw him again.

Soon, I was told that the promotions of the film were stalled as Irrfan wasn't well. In our crazy lives, we don't quite imagine something as drastic happening to people we know closely. We take things for granted and assume that they will always be as they are. It was not easy to come to terms or even imagine that Irrfan was suffering from a rare cancer.

This wasn't easy to digest. It doesn't happen like that. It doesn't happen to people like Irrfan. He was too engrossed in realizing those beautiful dreams that were all finally coming true, and he was in the midst of all that glory and more. He deserved to enjoy it, absorb it—this shouldn't have happened to him. And if it had happened, he should have been able to come out of it soon. He had come out of many a crisis, this would pass too, I thought. And he'll be back, he'll be fine . . . I was sure.

One kept hearing from common friends, reading news about him, but that charismatic gentleman with the shy smile kept his pain and suffering to himself. No one, except very close friends, really knew much. His beautiful, heart-wrenching writings on life and his journey with the illness came in the papers. It was heartbreaking to read one of his articles where he said, '. . . just when he had started enjoying the journey, the conductor had tapped on his shoulder and said, your destination is here. Get off.'

One hoped it would all just be a bad dream. He'd even shot for *Angrezi Medium*. I was happy the movies had got back their Irrfan. But then, the inevitable happened. During the crazy times amidst the lockdown, came the devastating news of his passing away. I was numb, sitting in front of the television, tears trickling down my face. His whole journey crossed my mind.

That man with those mesmerizing eyes, that man with that deep intense look which pierced through your soul, that man with that shy smile that would win a million hearts, that man whose silences spoke more than words could ever do, that man who everyone felt belonged to them . . . This was a personal loss for the entire nation.

Everyone mourned the passing away of a simple man with a crazy amount of talent who made it big on his own. Watching him on screen was like watching yourself, he was so relatable. I felt so helpless. Lockdown wouldn't allow me to say a final goodbye. I couldn't talk to Sutapa, his better half, who stood by him like a rock as she was in the midst of it all. *Who could I reach out to?* I spoke to all our common friends, but I was still very restless. In the night, as I was gathering myself up, I could just see his smiling face floating in front of my eyes.

But, dear Irrfan, I don't want to say that was that, this time.

I still want to hear the subtle jokes and grab them tightly with both my hands. I still want to react to that awesome actor standing in front of me whose eyes do all the talking, who makes everyone else speechless. I want to hear those silences, Irrfan. And I want to see that naughty glint in your eyes.

Cinema still hasn't had enough of you, and it will never be the same without you. And me? I'll miss my improvisations. I'll miss pulling my chair next to yours and saying thank you. I'll miss those magical moments of shooting with you, you marvellous man! I'll miss you weaving your magic on the screen like no one else could. I'll miss a super co-actor and an elusive friend.

And well, yes. That was that with Irrfan.

SALMAN KHAN

The song, *'Mere Rang Mein, Rangne Wali . . .'* was playing on the big screen. There was a lot of whistling in the huge theatre in Ludhiana. My friends and I had rushed post school to catch this latest romantic film, *Maine Pyar Kiya*. The new heart-throb was the talk of the town—and all girls were going crazy over him. I couldn't get enough of the stunningly good-looking hero dancing with the wind blowing on his face. Instant infatuation it was, and it lasted for a while. My room had Salman Khan's posters all over. I had bought all his postcards, and a few of them were used as bookmarks for my schoolbooks. In between classes, I would pull out his pictures and blush.

Imagine my ecstatic state when my mother told me that my director uncle, Deepak Bahry, was launching his new film in the summer holidays and the hero was Salman Khan. She had no idea what that piece of news had done to her daughter! I could actually meet my crush! I instantly put the tape recorder on and played, *'Mere Rang Mein, Rangne Wali . . .'*. 'Yes, I am coming my dear Salman . . . to meet you!' I said aloud as I danced.

I had already begun my preparations. The tailor was immediately told to stitch three dresses for me to choose from to wear at the mahurat. What if I looked so stunning that my uncle thought of casting me opposite Salman? After all, we'd all heard of girls being launched after they had been randomly spotted. I had finished shopping; the make-up and hairdo had been thought of, and with my extra full suitcase (only for the mahurat), we boarded the train to Mumbai.

On the way, we crossed the beautiful ghats of Igatpuri. I had begun daydreaming already—I was sprinting in my chiffon saree, and there stood Salman Khan, his hair flying in the wind, arms wide open for me as he sang, *'Mere Rang Mein, Rangne Wali . . .'*. And then, I heard a 'Cut'—my uncle had said cut to the shot! How I was hoping he would cast me with my heart-throb, through some twist of fate or a miracle.

In Mumbai, I couldn't wait for the day of the mahurat. In those days, the mahurat of a film was a huge affair. A scene would be enacted by the lead cast and a big celebrity would give the mahurat clap, and announce the film amongst a huge gathering of celebrity guests, press, family and friends.

I had chosen to wear a red organza dress which looked like a fairy's—all I needed was a magic wand. I went to the beauty parlour to get dressed up, and then, with the entire family, I reached the venue at a plush Pali Hill bungalow.

I took a seat in the first row so that it would be easier for Salman to spot me and tell my uncle, 'Why don't you cast that lovely girl in the red dress?' I waited with bated breath for him to appear on stage and notice me. In a few seconds, I saw him walk up the stage casually. Yes, in flesh and blood! Looking every inch the heart-throb that he was. The mahurat shot involved him and Gulshan Grover, and it happened smoothly amidst loud cheers. I guess he missed noticing me in the crowd, but I didn't give up hope.

So, I went up to my ever-dependable mother, insisting I had to meet Salman. She told my uncle about it (I was sulking because he still hadn't had the brilliant vision of his future heroine standing right in front of him). My uncle obliged and sent me with his man Friday to Salman. There he was, clicking pictures with the press. He had fake blood on the corner of his lips. I felt like going and wiping it (a la Suman from *Maine Pyar Kiya*).

'Hi!' I jumped in front of him, as if he would instantly recognize who I was. The press was a little taken aback, seeing this public display of exuberance. His eyes twinkled as if he'd burst into laughter, seeing this stranger jump in front of him from out of nowhere. The man Friday told him, '*Deepak sir ke bacche hain, photo khinchwa lo,* please sir (This is Deepak sir's kid. Can you oblige her with photographs?) If I could, I would have punched the man. How dare he call me a baccha? I was going to be Salman's future heroine! Bas, all Salman had to do was look at me attentively, but all he did was give me a faint smile and a photograph.

I don't think he even looked at me, as there were too many press people around. I had missed this chance of being spotted. I couldn't do anything more about it, so I left for home, heartbroken. Maybe another time. After all, dreams do come true.

And they did. when I finally entered the industry. My second film was *Veergati*. Again, it was harsh on my feelings for Salman. When I went to meet the director, he said, 'Salman is there in the film, and you . . . ' (I was hoping to hear the words that were long awaited. but I heard something that broke my heart instead). '. . . will play his sister!'

If I could, I would have screamed, 'Noooo!!!'

It was blasphemous. How could I play Salman's sister? In typical filmi fashion, I wanted to say, '*Nahiiiiin!!!! Ye nahin ho sakta!* (No, this can't be happening!)'

But well, I couldn't. I was a newcomer and the director had told me that it was a story about siblings. So, I thought of the positive side. Maybe after this film, Salman would think that the girl deserved to be his heroine and I'd get to do another film with him! With stars in my eyes and a bit of a heavy heart, I went on the sets of *Veergati* to be with my heart-throb.

The very first shot made me happy. Salman was to carry me to our house, the only problem being that I had to be a dead body (it was a revenge kind of scene—the sister had been killed by the villains and the brother was to take her body home and pledge revenge). First things first, I had to meet Salman. I was hoping he would not recognize me from that disastrous photo we had clicked. In any case, how could he? We had barely exchanged glances then.

There was a sudden flurry of activity on set. Everyone was wishing someone who had just arrived. Yes, it was Salman, casually walking straight to the set. This time, I didn't jump in front of him to introduce myself (my spirits were anyway low over playing this superstar's sister). I said a very meek hello, and the director introduced me to Salman. 'This is Divya Dutta, the new girl. She's playing your sister.' My heart had fully broken by now.

He looked at me, this time, intently. My heart skipped a beat, and then he broke into a smile, 'Hi Divya.' The song *'Mere Rang Mein, Rangne Wali . . .'* was about to play in my head when it was stopped short. The director intruded to explain the shot to him. 'So, your sister is dead, and you are carrying her body home.' The song in my head hit a huge pause button.

Salman put on his make-up on the set, and as the director announced 'Action!', he lifted me up. I had to shut my eyes, but I could hear him laugh. 'Cut, cut!' I heard.

I was wondering what had happened and I opened my eyes. 'Arey, you have to let your body loose, Divya. You are supposed to be dead!' shouted the director from far. I was embarrassed.

I looked at Salman who was still laughing. I couldn't help but laugh too, and his eyes looked very compassionate suddenly. 'Divya, when you act dead na . . . don't hold me. Let your body fall and I'll hold you. Trust me, I won't let you fall.'

Those words, on a different set, would have been music to my ears, although here too, they were very reassuring. So, in the second take, I let myself loose completely. Salman carried me, and as soon as he reached the assigned spot, he burst into peals of laughter. '*Arey baap re, bhaari hai yaar* (She's heavy),' he joked, leaving me embarrassed. But I saw his naughty eyes; he was putting me at ease. He was cracking jokes and was extremely protective.

I was getting to know Salman Khan outside of my infatuation zone, the real him. The compassionate and fun Salman. I can easily say he is one of the most supportive stars I have worked with—no airs, and a superb, subtle sense of humour. He would crack a joke under his breath, only for my ears, and I would burst into laughter, with the entire unit wondering what I had found so funny. Salman would then look at me poker-faced too, joining the unit with that same surprised look. His pranks were endearing, and I would often wonder if he was serious or joking.

One day, he called me aside after a shot and said, 'Come, I'll do a photoshoot for you.' That was very sudden. I was super excited but somewhere, I was wondering if he was pulling my leg. Not too sure as to what was in store, I followed him. He took out his camera. As I posed for my star, he took my pictures. It was like living a dream! Time had stopped. I could see him in slow motion, instructing me to change the angles. I was still sure he was playing a prank on me, but I was loving it nevertheless. As soon as we finished the shoot, we were called for our scene, and he became engrossed in it in no time.

I realized that Salman is a very intelligent actor. Knowing well what works for the audience, he delivers just that. And I would react to his subtle expressions. No doubt our scenes were turning out to be the highlight of the film.

One day, I faced a deadly problem (literally). We had already shot Salman carrying my dead body, but the cult scene of me falling off the window and breathing my last was yet to be shot. The only hitch being, that I continued to breathe even after 'dying'. I didn't know how to take a filmi last breath.

The director took a few takes. I thanked god that Salman had packed up and was leaving for the day, or I would have been crazy embarrassed. A few retakes had happened, but I was not prepared to die (pun intended). Unknown to me, an assistant went up to Salman as he was getting into his car and said, 'Sir, wo nayi ladki ko marna nahi aa raha! (The new girl doesn't know how to die!)' I'm sure he must have had that naughty twinkle in his eyes before he decided that he'd stay and help the 'nayi ladki'.

As I saw him re-enter the set, I froze. It would have ruined my so-far well-maintained reputation of doing scenes well and become so embarrassing. I was close to tears when he came and sat next to me on the ground. He told the unit to give us a few minutes. Then, he softly asked me what had happened. This time, I welled up, 'I am unable to die,' I said innocently and helplessly. He burst into uncontrollable laughter, so much so that his eyes started watering while I looked at him with a shocked expression. I felt I had jeopardized all my future chances of being his heroine.

In a few minutes, he composed himself and said, 'Divya, it's not tough, okay. Keep looking at me, I'll perform from a distance and you follow what I do. Okay? And when you shut your eyes, hold your breath for a while.'

'But I'll get suffocated, I am majorly claustrophobic,' I said. This time, he had a very warm smile on his face. 'All you have to do is count to ten, and then breathe again. If you do it well, the treat is on me.' Saying that, he lay on the dusty ground far from me, in a position that I could face the camera while looking at him. I had to get this right, I realized. He was taking such a lot of effort for a newcomer! As the director said, 'Action,' my eyes were on that one man only (that wasn't the tough part). I nervously followed what he was doing. He first enacted a fall from a height. I did the same. Then he gasped for breath. I followed him to the T. Then he took the last breath, and I did that too; shutting my eyes, holding my breath, feeling suffocated, but distracting myself by counting—one, two, three . . . But I could hold it no more.

Then I heard his voice in the distance, doing the count for me. '. . . seven, eight, nine, ten, and done!' Yes, I had done it. All thanks to this amazing co-star. How many people would come back from the car, and help a colleague to perform? Everyone cheered the two of us. This time, I jumped right in front of him, and hugged him tight. This time, there was no infatuation. This time, there was heartwarming gratitude.

To date, I fondly remember how nice he was to a newcomer. He made no big deal about what he had done and brushed the dust from his clothes, sat in his car and left, leaving behind an ever-thankful 'nayi ladki'.

The next day was my last day at shoot, and Salman's man Friday came and told me, 'Aaj lunch Salman bhai ke saath! (Today's lunch is with Salman!)' During lunch, his make-up room dining table was full of delicious food from home. 'Your treat,' he said. My god! *Did he always remember the minutest of things he promised?* We chatted, we laughed, and when I was leaving, I went up to him and emotionally uttered, 'Thank you for everything.' His naughty eyes twinkled again and he gestured to his man Friday, who got a packet for me. 'This is for you.' As I opened it, out came three T-shirts with my photographs on them—the ones Salman had clicked! *Did he always make such amazing gestures in the most unassuming way?*

I left that set a bit emotional, but with a bright smile and a hearty laugh, as he cracked a joke before I left. That's what I took back home too—go about doing everything you do but with a dash of humour, with a pinch of laughter. Every moment at work with Salman, I had a blast.

And that's what I do now. I remember to be me in between shots. I remember to smile and laugh. I remember to be there for cues to my co-actors and never leave it on ADs. And yes, I remember to be there for a newcomer. And this, I learnt from a man who held my hand and looked over me protectively, making each moment memorable, who gave me confidence when I needed it most, who literally took my breath away while teaching me how to die.

Even though I did not get to work with him again, I do a lot of things in ways that I inadvertently learnt from him . . . his hues sprinkled on my journey forward. Yes truly, I can still hear the song play in my head, 'Mere Rang Mein Rangne Wali . . .'

SRIRAM RAGHAVAN

His films have had me sitting on the edge of my seat. They were not only thrilling but extremely intelligently woven together, with plot lines that had one gasping for breath. I had absolutely loved *Johnny Gaddaar* and *Ek Haseena Thi*. His name would pop up and his work would widely be discussed in our common circles, but strangely, I never bumped into him at any parties or awards.

Sriram Raghavan is someone I remembered through a few of his pictures that appeared in newspapers. He clearly didn't seem to like the spotlight. However, one particular day, a newspaper write-up gave me an opportunity to meet this brilliant director and person extraordinaire.

My mornings, like many others, start with the newspaper; the minor difference being that since I am thoroughly obsessed with the Hindi film industry and a keen actor, I always pick the movie section first, and after scanning through the goings-on in the movie world, I go on to the other news sections. That eventful day, I came across a news item with a picture of Sriram Raghavan and Varun Dhawan. It immediately caught my eye. The headline mentioned that the director was looking out for a slightly older actress opposite Varun. I felt a surge of excitement. How I would love to be a part of *Badlapur*, but the hitch was that I didn't know him at all and neither did I have his number.

Even though a lot of work comes to me directly, I have never shied away from asking for it, if I really want to do a film. Strangely, without even knowing the script, I knew I really wanted to be a part of that film, and I couldn't really pinpoint a reason for thinking so. All I knew was I needed to connect with Sriram Raghavan. I quickly called my manager and asked her if I could get his number. After a long wait, the number was shared with me and I promptly sent him a message, asking for a good time to speak to him. I was not too sure what the response would be, as I thought he might be wary of talking to me since we didn't know each other personally at all.

But I was surprised, pleasantly at that, when after an hour or so, his name flashed on my phone. My heart did skip a beat, but I took the call instantly. As I said hi, a hurried but warm voice said, 'Hey, hi Divya, I just got your message. I am at a recce; can I call you in the evening please?'

I quickly replied, 'Yes, yes of course!'

What hit me first was the simplicity in that voice, no airs about who he was—humble, warm and with the familiarity that comes with knowing someone already. It instantly put me at ease, and brought a smile to my face. I thought he might not remember to call me, but he did. He called me in the evening and asked, 'Yes Divya, now I am free, tell me.'

Now that made me nervous, but I collected myself and uttered, 'So, I read this piece of news about you making *Badlapur*. I believe you are looking for an older actress opposite Varun, so I thought I must reach out as I would love to . . .' Phew! I had said it to someone I hadn't met ever. It felt a bit odd. There was silence on the other side too and on this side, I was sinking. He spoke politely, finally, 'So Divya, we are already considering a few actresses. Don't know why we didn't think of you, but let me give it a thought, I'll get back in a week.'

It was that honest, straightforward and genuine. No layering. He had just shared his thoughts with me as they were. In my experience in the industry, I had concluded that mostly no one says no to you on your face. They say, 'Sure, let's see,' and then that's the end of the story because they don't want to directly say no in an unpredictable industry, where you might need the same actor sometime. So, they opt for diplomacy instead (which is understandable). But this man was a breath of fresh air, he didn't seem sceptical about speaking the fact that he was already thinking of other actresses and yet, he was making a genuine attempt of at least giving it a thought. In a strange way, I felt very respected. Respected enough to be spoken the truth to—it was a straight stating of facts; it was that simple. I wondered why some people complicate things so much in their quest for diplomacy. This was so refreshing, and I felt so happy that I had at least put across my wish and the genuine man on the other side had promised to give it a thought. I knew he meant it; I could trust that voice instantly. I really didn't know what the outcome of this conversation would be, but as Ma used to say, 'Give it your best effort and then leave it to god.'

A week passed and I didn't still hear from him. I was sure he had cast someone else. I had just had a massive hit in *Bhaag Milkha Bhaag*, and because of that, I was the most popular sister in town, so, why would anyone risk casting me romantically opposite a heart-throb? I knew what I was capable of delivering, but one is mostly known by their previous work here, and you are cast likewise (I have always fought typecasting though), so I wouldn't blame him if he decided to go with someone else.

I was sad though because I wanted to work with Sriram Raghavan. I wanted to essay a different role, but alas, it was not to be. I tried distracting myself for a few days but my thoughts kept going back to *Badlapur*. It was an intuitive connect with the film and its maker. When I couldn't handle this barrage of thoughts, I gathered the courage to make one last call, one last try. The call was answered immediately and the same hurried voice said, 'Hey Divya, sorry ya, am still here. Why don't you come to office next week?' Same genuine warmth, but this time it left me guessing.

I had chewed all my manicured nails by the time the D-day arrived. I reached his office and the usher took me to his cabin. I opened the door and saw the man I had only seen in pictures. 'Hi Divya, please come.' A simple man with silver hair, he carried a certain depth in his being. My smile broadened on meeting him in person, never mind the heart thumping away in anticipation.

He introduced me to a very graceful lady sitting there. 'Meet Pooja Ladha Surti, the editor and co-writer of the film.' I liked her instantly—a person with a warm smile and a very intelligent disposition. A few matchboxes adorned his table, each one different from the other. He noticed me looking at them and said, 'I like collecting matchboxes,' and then suddenly added, '. . . so this film has four women and honestly, we had seen a few actors for this role, so . . .' I didn't want to hear the rest; I didn't want to hear the name of the actress they had finalized. I was close to shutting my eyes tight but refrained from doing so. The sensitive director that he is, he didn't keep the suspense for too long though. '. . . we all discussed it and we are happy to go with you for *Badlapur*!'

I now had to control that little tear from trickling out. He had believed in me, he had chosen to go with me despite so many choices—I think he had seen the hunger, the keenness.

In my attempt to keep breaking the image I was given with every release, *Badlapur* would prove to be very important for me after *Bhaag Milkha Bhaag's* sister act. This was a romantic lead, a surprise and a risk for the so-called market strategies, but Sriram had chosen to go with my faith in myself. He was ready to not follow the norms and invest in an actor who was eager to give her best. He had chosen to believe in me.

Yes, he was different, very different.

My first day of shoot was in Nashik jail with Nawazuddin Siddiqui (I was working with him for the first time too). It was intriguing to shoot in a real jail. I had seen it in so many films but it was the first time I was inside one, seeing a lot of real inmates in there too. Warily, I made my way to my unit people. In a prisoner's costume, at a distance, stood Nawaz.

I was introduced to Nawaz very casually by the very casual Sriram Raghavan, who always concentrates on his work, not the other nitty-gritties of social obligations. I knew he doesn't bother much about formalities, but comes straight to the point. So, Nawaz and I had the script in our hands, and I was waiting for Sriram to explain the shot and the position we were to take according to the camera placement. But he surprised me.

Sriram heard us read the lines and then asked, 'Okay, what would you like to do now, keeping the scene in mind?' 'Err . . .' I thought, '. . . why was he asking us that and not telling us what he wanted us to do?'

I got my answer in a few minutes. He was trying to see how we were naturally inclined to go about the scene first rather than restricting us with dos and don'ts. He wanted to give his actors ample freedom to perform without pressure, and was also involving them and seeking their inputs to the scene.

I later realized that Sriram is someone who believes in teamwork—giving each member their due and involving them in the feedback process, because knowing various perspectives expands your own vision and outlook. He had a crystal-clear vision as to what he wanted and yet, he was taking in all perspectives, in case he had missed out on something. What a positive and healthy way of working!

So, after we did a rehearsal, he choreographed the scene with the DoP, ace cinematographer Anil Mehta (who'd directed me earlier in *Aaja Nachle* too). Keeping the scene in mind and what we had done in the rehearsal, and of course, the camera angle, he came out with an extraordinary scene execution. Okay, so now I knew why *The* Sriram Raghavan is called extraordinary.

After that were my scenes with Varun Dhawan, and I remember I delivered some poetic lines in a very poetic way (in my heart thinking that was a good recital), until Sriram quietly came to me and whispered, 'Divya, the lines are already saying it, so don't emphasize, say them straight.' That hit home with a bang. He was right, and I said those lines straight (this time I realized that it did sound way better!).

After that, I never forgot that simple mantra. Be truthful to the lines, support them when they are conveying what they have to. One doesn't have to try too hard with modulations. Sometimes, just being simple is the magic formula.

The outdoor shoot went like a breeze. In the Mumbai schedule was the famous kissing scene with Varun. I realized Sriram is a shy man. He just came and called Varun and me for a briefing, explaining very well what exactly he wanted from that scene—the nuances, the purpose of Varun's visit, my vulnerability—everything. And then, he matter-of-factly added, 'The rest … you guys do what's comfortable.' Varun and I smiled at his sweet way of telling us to do the intimate scene, keeping the undercurrents in mind.

The film went on to become a blockbuster. To celebrate it, I went to meet Sriram and Pooja at the office.

What was supposed to be just a courtesy meet turned out to be an evening to remember. Someone has rightly said, the best things in life happen impromptu, and the best moments in life are often unplanned. We were just randomly discussing music and old classics (I have a particular attachment to old songs as I have seen my parents listen to them and have hummed them throughout my childhood). So, every time Sriram, Pooja and I discussed a song, one of them would narrate an anecdote related to the song and regale me with all the details of the singer, music director, actors, etc. and the stories behind the songs. And then, Sriram would play the song on his laptop. Some things can't be explained in words but what I felt that evening was sheer joy. Three people bonding over old films, music, actors, and singing those songs together—that, for me, was the beginning of a beautiful friendship with Sriram Raghavan, Pooja Ladha Surti and also producer Sanjay, whose office is our hub. In our field, where people mostly meet to discuss work, we not only did that but had these rarely-heard-of fun evenings too.

One day, I invited Sriram and the entire crew of *Badlapur* home for dinner and music. All Punjabi delicacies were prepared as Sriram loves food (it's a different thing that he doesn't eat much). Everything was ready and I got a call from Sriram. 'Accha listen, Divya, I forgot there's a launch party by my producers and I'll have to go there for a bit, so I may be a little late.' I didn't say anything, but normally, when we say 'in a bit,' it means it can extend to a few hours. So, I was mentally prepared that my get-together would easily be delayed by two hours.

So, I sat watching a random film, while I was waiting for them. In about twenty minutes, the doorbell rang, and the entire crew along with Sriram was there! 'Did you not go?' I asked, utterly surprised.

'I did, but quickly said hi and came. I had promised na, so can't be late,' he said matter-of-factly again. I stood smiling for a bit.

Here was a man, untouched by the filmi code of conduct (of socializing, etc.). He was a man of his word and did what he thought was the right thing to do. His simplicity and humility are endearing, almost to a point that I'd probably feel protective of him. Everything about him is simple. Everything is said simply. *Isn't life easier and more beautiful when simple?* No complications. It's so refreshing to meet a man totally unaffected by his own success and stature, who goes about his work just as simply, adding a huge dose of his passion to his work. But outside of it, he's a man who loves cinema, old classics, music, books, and food, not necessarily in that order. He takes his work very seriously but not himself, and that I think is a huge feat to achieve, but to him, it comes naturally.

Well, so the crew got themselves comfortable and amidst the Punjabi food being served, the karaoke mic was taken over by Sriram and a fun evening began in earnest. No one in that room, at that moment, was an actor, director, writer or editor any more—we were all like an excited bunch of kids, bonding over old songs—someone singing, some playing tabla on the table, some dancing, all living that moment to the fullest. A beautiful evening indeed with some beautiful people!

Much later, when I bumped into that big producer whose launch Sriram had just made a quick appearance at, to be at my get-together, he remembered to ask me, 'So what was the occasion at your place the other day that the entire crew with Sriram just left in a hurry to be there? *Humein toh bulaya nahi aapne?* (You didn't invite me?)' I just had a broad grin on my face 'for a bit' and felt a lot of affection for Sriram.

Sometime later, I got a call from Sriram. 'Come, a few of us are getting together. I'll narrate a story. Need your feedback.' It felt really nice. Normally, story narrations are limited to the immediate crew of writers, director, assistant directors, etc., but here was a man who likes to take opinions of people with different perspectives. I went to the office and a bunch of people were already seated there—one more actor, Pooja, Sanjay and the DoP, Mohanan. Sriram said he was going to narrate a story and would want honest feedback. The story was of *Andhadhun* (untitled at that time). We all sat in pin-drop silence and heard Sriram narrate, in his super casual style, painting a picture of the scenes as he explained each movement, each nuance. After about two hours, he broke the spell, as he told us that was the end. 'What? Really?' Everyone gasped at the shock value of the climax. But before we could give our reactions, he said, '*Chalo* let's chill first. We'll take a break, then discuss.'

We ate, we heard old songs and then we were back to work. I was really enjoying this part of movie-making I had never experienced. I am mostly given a fully bound script before the shoot, all ready. Here, I was part of it right from its inception— discussing scenes, giving my points of view, hearing what others had to say. What an extremely enjoyable, healthy process of working—taking everyone's opinion and then making decisions on what fits the script! It was an amazing way to check if there was a point of view he had missed while writing. Everything was covered in the discussions, right from the story, the climax, the casting, and the title of the film. Everything. And I felt so connected with the entire process. Imagine being a part of casting and suggesting names (an absolute first for me and an absolute pleasure too).

Even though I didn't do *Andhadhun* (Sriram was kind enough to offer), I was an integral part of it, right from these sessions, to its previews and to it getting the National Award while I hosted the ceremony and announced the award. This connect with a film I wasn't a part of was a first for me and very surreal, and I owe this amazing experience and a novel learning process to Sriram.

Sriram has always suggested that I write a script, and I have always loved his confidence in me. Maybe, someday I will.

Post the lockdown, the first thing I did was ask Sriram, Pooja and Sanjay if I could meet them. I was missing the fun evenings. I can't explain the feeling of sheer delight when I saw them. It was like meeting family, like getting together with soul friends. It was back to old music (my connect with my parents' choice of music kept alive by these lovely people). As Sriram excitedly said, '*Chal*, guess who's singing this song. Do you know it's Nutan ji?' My heart was jumping with joy—to be with people I love and do what I love doing! Exactly the Sriram Raghavan way.

As I sat there listening to yet another beautiful narration, being an integral part of it yet again, I just thought I wanted to hold on to that moment forever. I've been fortunate to keep such amazing experiences in my bag of memories that I'll cherish all my life. Of learning so subtly from a wizard; of enjoying these golden moments not many can boast of, of hearing amazing stories and being a part of them.

Well, here's raising a toast to you Sriram, for being the golden-hearted man that you are; for the simplicity that adorns you; for being the most real human being I know; for the lovely jam sessions; for being one of the finest in your craft; for your stories; for the music, and for that precious book on songs and the stories behind them, Gaata Rahe Mera Dil, that you gifted me with a handwritten note: 'Here's to many singing moments.'

Yes to many signing (movies with you) and singing moments, because this film journey has been much brighter with you in it.

GURDAS MAAN

In my growing up days, I had often heard from Ma about a young man who had become a star with his songs and performances. She'd told me that '*Dil Da Mamla Hai*' and '*Mamla Gadbad Hai*' were his most popular songs. And then, I saw him on television for the first time in a traditional Punjabi outfit with a *dafli* in his hand. The handsome man performed like a dream! There was so much energy in his performance and the ability to make his audience get up and dance to his tunes. Literally!

I first met Gurdas Maan, thanks to his wife Manjeet Maan, who was producing a Punjabi film, *Shaheed-e-Mohabbat*. After *Train to Pakistan* released, I got a call from her. She had seen the film and wanted to cast me opposite her husband in a cross-border love story, where a man falls in love with a child-woman and sacrifices his life for her. It was a beautiful love story and Manjeet ji was very clear that she wanted the *Train to Pakistan* girl in it.

When I was told I would be cast opposite Gurdas Maan in the film, I was filled with child-like excitement. I knew my mom would be the happiest! After all, to say 'My girl is working with *the* Gurdas Maan,' would be a huge feat in a place where everyone was curious about what the Doctor saab's daughter was up to in the movie world! This bit of news would surely put any scepticism to rest.

Finally, I met him on the sets of the film, which was in a village on the outskirts of Chandigarh. He came and met me with a humility I hadn't seen thus far. He bowed his head in front of Ma and me and then held my hand to his forehead (as if in absolute reverence). I was totally taken by surprise! I was the one who looked up to him and he was the one making me feel so respected! He spoke to me in *thet* (staunch) Punjabi. Honestly, despite having lived in Punjab, my Punjabi was the kind spoken in cities and it took me a while to understand that lingo. It was like music to the ears—I surely wanted to speak like him.

My mother took over and started chatting with him and telling him all about when she had first seen him perform on stage. She had also visited Sai ji, the revered saint whose dargah is in Nakodar, Jalandhar. Maan saab, as he's fondly called by everyone, is a huge devotee. Ma told him about Sai ji's prediction when she had gone to pay obeisance to him. '*Gurdas naal kamm karugi teri kudi* (Your daughter will work with Gurdas).' And, it had finally come true.

It was on those very sets where I first met my producer— Manjeet Maan ji—a warm, affable and self-assured woman, who was the reason I was in that film and my late director, the fabulous Manoj Punj, who also directed me in two more of Maan saab's films. I instantly felt at home due to their warmth. Since it was my third film, I was still learning the ropes and discovering my role as Zainab, the child-woman. What I learnt throughout the shoot though, was that everyone on that set was taken care of extremely well and quite well-fed or rather overfed, thanks to Manjeet ji and Maan saab! I soon became the baccha of the set and Manoj would fondly call me *Gudiya* (doll).

One day, we were in the middle of a tough shot and I was memorizing my dialogues. Just then, some local boys came running in. 'Madam ji, autograph *de do ji*!' they said excitedly. I was so into my lines that I brushed them aside saying, '*Baad mein aana, please* (Come later).' They went away, sad-faced.

When I was done with my lines, I finally looked up and saw the boys beaming with happiness and jumping around someone. As one of the boys moved, I saw that they were with Maan saab. He was greeting one of them in a similar manner that he had welcomed me with. The glow of happiness on the boys' faces was unparalleled.

When I went for the shot, I asked him out of sheer curiosity, 'Don't you get distracted when you meet people in between a tough shot?'

He looked at me and smiled. 'They are the ones who make us who we are. They are our audience and they love us. How long does it take anyway to bring a smile to their faces? Not even thirty seconds. It doesn't distract me for sure. In fact, their positive vibes help me perform better.'

The shot went off very well but his words kept playing in my head. I was feeling bad for the boys who went away with sad faces when I declined to give them an autograph. I quickly sent my man Friday to look for them. They were about to get on their cycles and ride back home but my man Friday caught them in time. They had a bewildered look on their faces when they were brought to me. I apologized quickly. '*Sorry, mera poora dhyan dialogues mein tha. Aa jao, autograph dun* (I was concentrating on my dialogues. Let me sign your autographs now).' Their faces lit up instantly. I asked my man Friday to get them some hot chai and we chatted for a bit. When those boys left, they were absolutely ecstatic.

Maan saab was right. This gesture had made their day and I had three more people who were now my fans for life. Something within felt so light and beautiful and I had this one man to thank for it.

Today, I don't refuse a single fan. I make sure to take the effort to make their day special. Maan saab's words reverberate in my ears till date. 'It doesn't even take thirty seconds to do that.'

Shaheed-e-Mohabbat went on to become a big hit, not only among Punjabi audiences but across the world. I remember famous single-screen theatres in Mumbai like Gaiety–Galaxy getting sold out because of a Punjabi film! The film went on to win many national awards too. It also opened up the gates of the Hindi film industry for me. And Gurdas Maan and Manjeet Maan's house became my go-to place in Mumbai after that. When you live away from home, the tinge of familiar warmth coming from somewhere is always welcome and very reassuring. I would often have meals with them and experience the hospitality of these exceptional hosts. I felt I had a home in Mumbai too where I could just walk in unannounced like a child.

I did three more films with Maan saab and Manjeet ji.

The shoot for *Des Hoyaa Pardes* was among my most memorable ones. Shooting a fabulous script with your own people—it couldn't have been better! I remember Manjeet ji had told me, 'Some would think that it's blasphemous to cast the superhit jodi of *Shaheed-e-Mohabbat* as siblings in the next, but I really want you to do this role.' Her clarity and conviction were enough for me to be the superstar's sister in his next film. Maan saab was a huge help in getting me into character for the kid sister's role.

I realized Maan saab is an absolute natural. He would be himself before the shot, either chatting or just being in his quiet zone, but as soon as the director said 'Action!', he would immediately get into character. Absolutely effortlessly. His inherent goodness added an innocence to his role which helped me as a co-actor in the bargain.

In this film, my Punjabi was as pure as his. I had learnt it from him by just observing, listening and spending time with him in his house. I had become a pro. I remember one of the scenes that we shot for vividly. I'll never forget it. It was a scene where the brother-sister duo was being tortured. In the scene, the sister (me) is being verbally abused and molested, and the brother, despite being tortured himself, attempts to protect his sister. The genuineness with which he did that scene, I honestly felt there was an elder brother actually doing that for his sister. The hangover of the hit romantic jodi melted away that day.

I have come to realize that Maan saab is extremely spiritual. He's with the world and yet in his own. He isn't even bothered about what role he is playing and with whom. He only concentrates on what he is asked to do and does it with all his heart. No questions asked. Simple.

Manjeet ji had another ace up her sleeve when she offered me *Waris Shah: Ishq Daa Waaris*, one of the grandest films made in Punjab with Gurdas Maan in the titular role. She had the same smile of conviction when she told me that I was to play a woman in love with Waris. The woman's feelings are not reciprocated, and she turns grey, a fabulous role with a superb graph. I joked with her, 'You have made me portray all possible relationships with Maan saab! First his beloved, then sister and now the other woman!'

'Well, I think you can pull them all off!' she replied with a smile.

Playing a seductress in this one was a challenge for me. At the same time, playing such a variety of roles with one actor was putting me in an interesting space. During *Waris Shah*, I saw Maan saab's spiritual side more often. When he would sing 'Heer', it seemed as if he was meditating on it. Since he was a poet himself and a spiritual one at that, playing Waris Shah seemed easy for him. Sometimes, I couldn't make out the difference between Maan saab and the character he was portraying. They both merged somewhere beautifully.

Even off the shoot, Maan saab's approach to life has been very philosophical. To every happy news or sad one, his reaction has always been, '*Sai meher kare . . .*' Leaving it all in the hands of the almighty and yet doing one's own karma is what he has always advocated.

The interesting thing about meeting Maan saab is getting to see different sides of him in different situations. At home or when we meet at a get-together with friends, his sense of humour is unparalleled. If he's comfortable with the people he's with, Maan saab is full of anecdotes and jokes and a superb wit. At work, on the other side, he brings along a lot of professionalism and a certain quiet around him.

On stage, he's a wonder. I recently went to Sai ji's annual mela in Nakodar, where Maan saab also performs every year. I wanted to go and pay my obeisance at the dargah; experience the festivities and witness Maan saab's performance. After darshan, I was guided to the area where Maan saab was going to perform and I was astounded to see thousands of people gathered there from various places. Some of them had been there since the previous night to get a seat and see Maan saab in action. There was a loud cheer as he got up on stage, clad in a yellow traditional Punjabi outfit and a dafli in his hand. He looked like a dream. The moment he started to sing, play the dafli and tap his feet, the crowd went berserk.

He stopped in between to thank his audience and a few of us who were present there! That's his way of humbly acknowledging people who had come to see his performance. He then began tapping his feet and playing his dafli again, and there was no stopping him! It was like some divine energy was within him to perform non-stop. It felt like he got more energy from performing. The audience just couldn't get enough of him! It was a marvel that could only be seen to be believed. Just like Ma had described it many years ago. Some things never change. Gurdas Maan continues to weave his magic on his audience, which includes me.

Back in Mumbai, their house still is home to me. They always honour their word. I remember requesting him to do a play with me and also to perform at the annual Prithvi Theatre Festival (as requested by Kunal Kapoor, the owner of Prithvi). He and Manjeet ji agreed to do both, since I am their *ghar ki ladki* and they'd never say no to me. That sense of belonging and being able to say something *haq se* is a true blessing. And I must say I am truly blessed.

I remember taking my four-year-old nephew to meet him. The first time Vehaant met him, he fell in love with his 'Maan saab uncle' because he made an effort to make him feel at home—playing hide-and-seek with him while the rest of us looked at the two of them in awe.

For my nephew, he's the favourite uncle, and as Maan saab had said, 'How long does it take to bring that smile on someone's face?' Sure! The little child is his fan for life and well . . . so am I. A big fan of this thorough gentleman, who's really god's own man.

And to him, I'll say in his own words, 'Sai meher kare!'

RISHI KAPOOR

I always had a soft corner for Rishi Kapoor. I loved his acting and his songs, and his hit jodi with Neetu Singh. There hasn't been a single time when his songs have played and I haven't danced. There was something magnetic about his screen presence. For me, he was the evergreen lover boy— his expressions when he sang a romantic number, that bright smile which reached his eyes, and his effortless dancing. He was a joy to watch and I absolutely adored him.

I first met Rishi Kapoor on the sets of *Delhi-6*. As mentioned earlier, the entire cast, Waheeda Rehman, Rishi ji, Abhishek, Atul Kulkarni, Sonam Kapoor, Om Puri, and I were staying at a resort on the outskirts of Jaipur. Each one of us had our own little bungalow-like cottage within the resort, but the place for having lunch and dinner was common. That is where I saw him.

He was having a word with the director, Rakeysh Omprakash Mehra. I was so thrilled to see him! Rakeysh ji introduced us and Rishi ji warmly met me. But I wanted to really celebrate meeting him for the first time. So, I went up to one of the assistant directors who played the guitar and together, with a few other actors, we started singing all of Rishi Kapoor's songs while walking from my cottage to the base where Rishi ji was still sitting. I must say, he was pleasantly surprised to see a caravan of youngsters coming towards him singing his songs. He too started cheering us. We all ended the session with 'Main Shayar Toh Nahin . . . (I'm Not a Poet)' and bowed down to him. 'Welcome to the set, sir! We love you!' we shouted out in unison.

Yes, he was overwhelmed.

He had this amazing quality about him—his child-like transparency. Whatever he was feeling within, reflected outside. We could all see he was moved by this gesture, and he gave me a hug.

We were shooting in the nights for the climax of the film. We used to sit together around a heater in the waiting area and chat until we were called for our shot in the cold, wintry nights. During one such conversation, we got to know that Rishi ji had never done a film that required shooting at night since he hated night shoots, and that *Delhi-6* was the first one. And although he hated the late-night shooting, he would still be his jovial self and narrate fun anecdotes about what had happened on a particular shoot, or how he shot a certain scene—and the way he narrated felt so warm and personal, as if he had known you for ever and was very comfortable sharing the story with you. There was an inherent warmth about him, and I just loved the way he sulked in a child-like way if he was made to wait for too long at night.

Those night shoots helped me bond beautifully with Chintu ji (as he was fondly called). We later met at Bachchan saab's Diwali party, where he said with all his heart, '*Yaar tere saath kaam karna hai! Accha sa!* (Would love to do good work with you!)'

He did a guest appearance in *Chalk and Duster*, which also had Shabana Azmi and Juhi Chawla. We were shooting for the climax of the film and I was delighted to be shooting with him again. He would excitedly share how he was enjoying this new phase in his career where he was doing varied roles. His films *Agneepath*, *D–Day* and the yet-to-be released at that time, *Kapoor & Sons* (where he had to sit for his make-up for four hours every day to play the grandfather) were great examples of the vast variety of characters he was portraying. He was happy that he was finally doing roles that were so different from his earlier romantic leads. He looked like a satiated actor but, at the same time, super excited to discover more.

During the shoot of the climax, Ma had fallen ill and I happened to share this with Shabana ji and Rishi sir. He sensed my apprehension about taking Ma for surgery and very matter-of-factly said, '*Aajkal toh fatafat ho jaata hai, jao aur karwa ke aa jaao yaar* (These days surgery is very quick. Go get it done and come back).' His words gave me strength and reassurance at that time.

Later, his film *Mulk* was released and everyone was raving about the amazing role he had essayed. I too sent him a message to congratulate him. As always, he was very prompt in replying and sounded happy. He later sent me his book and a message, '*Zaroor padhna* (You must read it).'

Then one day, I heard from someone that Rishi sir was not well and that he had flown to New York for treatment. Sometimes, you feel these drastic things do not happen to people you are close to. So, I couldn't really digest that piece of news about this adorable man, who was so full of life and lived it like a king. I sent him a message to check on him and he sent me a very funny and witty reply.

He was taking this challenge life had thrown at him head-on and with a smile (with the able support of Neetu ji and the rest of his family, of course). They all seemed very positive. And then, I saw an interview of Rishi ji with Neetu ji in New York, where he was talking about his plans when he returned to India. Yes, he was excited to get back and take on all the movies that were waiting for him to be a part of them! The twinkle in his eyes while he said it was heart-warming, and I choked watching this legend's zest for life and his work.

In November, there is an annual celebration at the Prithvi Theatre, and as Kunal Kapoor was very keen, I had requested Gurdas Maan to perform there. The theatre was crowded, but thankfully, I had got myself a good seat. As I turned back to check on the familiar faces present there, I saw Rishi ji sitting right behind me! I can't explain my joy on seeing him! We waved at each other!

As soon as the show finished, I ran to meet him and gave him a big hug. 'How are you, sir?'

He had a warm smile and that child-like excitement was still intact. 'I am back! All well. *Ab bas kaam shuru karunga. Yaar tere sath ek acchi film karni hai!* (Now, I will just start work. Need to do a good film with you!)' I was overwhelmed and delighted to have him back; knowing that he would be back to doing what he loved most. 'Welcome back, sir! Great to have you back,' I said. (The welcome that we had put together for him on the sets of *Delhi-6* flashed before me and I felt a sense of déjà vu).

Yes, I absolutely adored him and couldn't wait to work with him again.

Talks were on for a film and the director told me, 'Rishi ji is in the film and he was very happy when I told him you are being considered for one of the key roles.' I was looking forward too, to be on the sets with him again, and then, the COVID-19 lockdown happened.

I used to keep following him on Twitter. I absolutely loved and enjoyed his posts. It all seemed fine, until catastrophe struck. Irrfan's passing came as a big blow to everyone, and in just a few days, the sudden passing of Rishi sir came as a shock! But how could it be? He seemed fine . . . a thousand thoughts clouded my head. What didn't come was acceptance. That man, who lived life the way it should have been lived, in true style, was gone!

We couldn't pay our last respects because of the lockdown. The family had very gracefully requested everyone to pay their tributes from home. His songs were continuously playing on all news channels—'*Aur thodi der mei bas, hum juda ho jayenge* (We will be separated in a bit).' And I had tears in my eyes.

You are badly missed, Chintu ji. There was a lot more of you to still see and cherish, but yes, you have left us with the legacy of your amazing work which will last us a lifetime! I sit writing this and watching 'Jeevan ke din chote sahi, hum bhi bade dilwale (There are few days in life, but our hearts are magnanimous)' and I smile, remembering you. Here's celebrating you and your inimitable spirit, Rishi sir. Your smile that reached the eyes, your brilliance, your effortless steps, your child-like zest for life . . .

One thing shall remain unchanged . . . I absolutely adore you sir, now and always!

JACKIE SHROFF

He is undoubtedly a thorough gentleman and one of the most genuine and humble human beings I have met. Not to miss mentioning his amazing personality, swag and a straightforwardness that is rare! Yes, he is one in a million, with a golden heart—Jackie Shroff, fondly called Jaggu dada.

Back in my school days, his posters used to adorn the walls of my room and we all used to discuss how stylish he looked in just about anything he wore. But what I liked the most about him was his smile . . . straight from the heart.

I met him for the first time on the set of a film. I wasn't acting in the film, just as yet. The producer of that film had promised though and he had called me and my manager on the sets at a Madh Island bungalow. The unit was setting up a shot. It was very crowded and I stood alone outside as my manager went to look for the producer. I was feeling a bit lost. Suddenly, there was a lot of commotion behind me. As I turned, I saw Jaggu dada walking on to the set briskly, more handsome and stylish in person than I had imagined. I gasped just looking at him; raised my hand mid-air to try and wave at him. He waved back as he moved past me. I kept staring at him.

To my utter surprise, he suddenly stopped and turned around. 'Hi, can I help you? Are you waiting for someone?' My heart skipped a thousand beats. 'Hi!' I blurted. 'No sir, I came to meet the producer. I am doing this film, so my manager has gone inside . . .' and I quickly added, '. . . it's so good to see you!'

By now, he was fully focused on me and so were the rest of the unit members accompanying him. He asked his man Friday to pull up two chairs and sat with me. I couldn't believe that this star—for whom everyone was waiting inside—had stopped by to make a rank newcomer he didn't even know, feel comfortable. He had been perceptive enough to gauge that I was feeling lost. I didn't realize that he was guiding me protectively too. '*Chai peeyega, bidu?* (Will you have tea, buddy?)' he asked in his patent style and before I could reply, he told his assistant, '*Do cutting chai la, bidu* (get two cups of tea).' I nervously introduced myself to him. He was very warm and casual—making me feel absolutely comfortable—so much so that the unit people too were wondering, '*Ye ladki kaun hai?* (Who's this girl?)'

Then he quietly asked, 'Bidu, have you been signed for this film?'

I answered excitedly and naively, 'No . . . but the producer said he will and called us . . .'

He held my arm and said, 'As far as I know, they have signed up someone yesterday . . . so just be sure of these things and don't believe anything until you sign. Ever. *Ye hamesha yaad rakhna, baccha* (remember this, kiddo). *Theek hai?*' and he left, waving at me.

I sat with my cutting chai, staring in the direction he had gone long after he had left.

In a world full of diplomacy, where everyone wants to be politically correct or would rather not say anything, here was a guy giving such sound advice to someone he didn't know at all! And so protectively!

I had a smile on my face even though I should have been heartbroken to hear that someone else had already been signed up. When my manager came out with the producer, I confidently asked him, 'Sir, when will you be signing me for the film?' My manager looked zapped! She tried stopping me but I wanted clarity. For my sake. Even if that meant displeasing a producer who had already kept me on hold for so long.

'*Batata hun jaldi* (I will tell you soon) . . .' he mumbled. But this time, I had the sound advice of my senior which had filled me with a confidence I really needed at that point of time! Showing no desperation of any kind, I said with confidence, 'Sir, if I am doing the film, please tell us today and give us the signing amount. I would so love to do the film, but please don't waste our time. We've waited so long already.' All the frustration of having to keep calling him to check if I was doing the film came out in a very graceful manner.

I must say that I was proud of myself and something felt light inside too! All thanks to someone who just came and instilled that confidence in me, without even being aware of it. And that is the magnanimity of this awesome man, a real-life hero.

The first film I shot with him was *Agni Sakshi*, where I played Manisha Koirala's sister. I had been cast in the film as the makers thought I bore a distinct resemblance to Manisha. I didn't share too much screen space with Jackie, except for one scene, but I was so excited to meet him. I was still so grateful! When I went up to meet him, he was his usual warm self. I couldn't refrain from reminding him about the incident. He just laughed, '*Aur sab bhalo?* (All good?)' For some reason, he always thinks I am Bengali although I have told him about my Punjabi roots.

My next film with him, where I shared considerable screen space with dada, was *Chehere*. I had some romantic scenes with him and he made sure I was extremely comfortable. I was floored and absolutely charmed by his chivalry and caring nature.

It's the most beautiful feeling in the whole world to be looked after even if you are an independent person. He always made sure the lady was well taken care of. He would open the door of the car and see me off to make sure I left safely! How many people have the time or inclination to do that? I admire him immensely for that.

On the sets of Dev saab's movie, *Chargesheet* (which I have mentioned in Dev saab's chapter) I saw another side of Jaggu dada—the *bindaas* bidu.

Everyone knows of his absolute love for Dev saab since Dev saab had launched him in *Swami Dada*. The sweet and sensitive man that Jaggu dada is, he had been ever so grateful to Dev saab, even for that cameo! As I got to the set, I greeted Jaggu dada warmly and we chatted for a while. He is always in such a positive frame of mind! I mentioned something that was bothering me and he just laughed it off. '*Arey parwah nai karne ka bidu! Bindaas rehne ka, apna kaam karne ka bas. Life hai! Mast rehne ka!* (Don't worry, live life to the fullest and do your job. Stay happy!)' Truer words have not been said. Coming from someone who has gone through a lot to reach where he has, with honesty and hard work, they are even more precious! And yes, he practises what he preaches—he is always mast, celebrating life.

On the set, everyone was in their vanity vans, but Jaggu dada lay on the bonnet of his car with his legs crossed; listening to Dev Anand songs with his eyes shut, immersed in his own world, not bothered about the goings-on around. That I think is meditation in itself. He's never been bothered about typical filmi idiosyncrasies; he's never been bothered if someone else has had a better line or role. He would, in fact, laud and encourage them, and he'd be the happiest if someone performed well, as if it was his own personal victory!

He is wonderfully secure in his own self. Subhash Ghai, who actually launched Jackie Shroff as the lead in his film, *Hero*, had shared a very interesting anecdote on a television show. He had related that when he finalized Jackie for the film and told him so, Jackie, instead of being excited about it, had gone up to him to share that he had done a cameo in *Swami Dada*. That was because more than bagging a hero's role in the biggest film of the time, it was more important for him to not hide facts and be honest. He didn't want the producer to put high stakes on him and lose. This attitude of his led him to win hearts and the film in the bargain.

I'll never forget the time when we were in Goa for the International Film Festival of India's (IFFI) annual event. The welcome party was attended by top ministers and many stars. After meeting everyone, I tried to leave early since it was very crowded. I was making calls to my driver and trying to find my team members in that crowd. Jaggu da was sitting right in front of me. He got up, came and stood beside me, held my hand and led me to the exit. '*Chal aa bidu*,' he said taking me along, '. . . *tere ko tera gaadi mei bithaon. Bahut rush hai* (Let me help you get to your car, it's too crowded).' His protective grip on my hand overwhelmed me. I was so touched by his gesture that I couldn't even open my mouth to say thank you. I just watched as he briskly walked back, waving at me, after making sure I safely sat in my car. As always, I was left with that familiar feeling I always experience when I am with him—of being taken care of.

Thank you, Jaggu da! Your inherent goodness touches a lot of hearts, mine included! And in real life, I will always sing '. . . Tu Mera Hero Hai . . .! (You are my hero!)'

SONALI BENDRE

The news had shaken me up. People you make your beginnings with are so, so special. And Sonali Bendre is someone who's very special to me. I had just read the devastating news of her being diagnosed with cancer and it left me shocked to the core, and nostalgic of our past together.

Years ago, after being selected for the Stardust Academy, Ma had come to drop me to the bungalow in Mumbai which was supposed to be my house for the next three months, along with six more youngsters—two girls and four boys. We had been selected out of 50,000 candidates all over India to be trained to become actors.

As I set my foot in the lobby, a lovely girl with an angelic face extended her hand warmly and said chirpily, 'Hi, I am Sonali Bendre.' I was dazed. How could anyone be that pretty? She most definitely was the loveliest of them all!

She didn't wait for any help to arrive, and on seeing me look clueless, took my bags inside and showed me the room. 'You can share my room. I think we can be good friends,' she smiled. I looked around at the neatly done up room, trying to get acclimatized to the newness of it all. Leaving home, coming to a new place, and this stunner in front of me—it was all very overwhelming. I looked at her again, this time, for a little longer—she was innocent-looking with angelic eyes and drop-dead-gorgeous looks, tall, thin and had silky long hair: like someone straight out of a fairy tale. When Ma used to describe a fairy in her stories, she must have been like Sonali.

I was apprehensive to even strike a conversation with her. How do such beautiful people talk? I felt like a mere mortal for a few days, and would keep my distance from this stunner who I couldn't get myself to talk to, except reply in monosyllables to whatever she asked me. If she was amused, well, she didn't show it.

I opened up with her in the acting classes. We were mostly paired together to perform and I saw that she made sure I was very comfortable. We both used to improvise a lot in our acts, and for that, one needs to know the other's timing, and both need to have good chemistry to react to whatever the other actor throws instantly at you. We both had mastered that. Everyone, including the teachers, would look forward to our acts.

Gradually, I started opening up. We started having conversations about home, parents, dreams, aspirations, the boys in our batch, typical girly talk and more. There was another girl with us too, Indrani, but she chose to keep to herself and we didn't disturb her much.

Sonali was very protective of me, like an elder sister. Being a staunch Punjaban, I loved to have milk at night. Call it the habits Ma had inculcated, but I had a strong urge to have a glass of milk every night. No one else seemed to want it though, nor was there any left by the end of the day. I used to sneak into the kitchen every night to look for some leftover milk. One day, I discovered milk powder packs in the kitchen cupboard. Delighted, I fixed myself up a nice, big glass, and drank to my heart's content.

It gradually became a norm. I would tiptoe into the kitchen, sneak out the powder and bring it to my room. The only person who knew about it was Sonali. When I had offered some to her, she had patted my cheek and said, '*Tu pi le* (You have it).' And I did.

One fine day, the expected happened. Someone reported the disappearance of the packets to the matron in the bungalow. She summoned all of us down, and the questioning started. I was nervous. I knew I would be caught and publicly shamed. I held Sonali's wrist tight, but she didn't even look at me. *Would she give me away?*

I was even more nervous, when I heard the matron shout, 'I am asking one last time!' A voice interrupted her. The assertive, confident voice of the girl standing next to me. 'I took it for Divya every night. What is the big deal? She's used to having milk every night, and you guys don't keep milk in the fridge at night. So, I found these packets and gave her some,' she said matter-of-factly, taking it all on herself. And then her tone changed to a very polite one, 'Wouldn't you do that too, ma'am, if a child wants milk? I thought you'd be happy that I'm taking care of her, just as you would like it.' The matron's expression changed too. She instantly softened. 'Yes, of course. Good you did that. In fact, I'll tell Ramu to keep some extra milk for Divya every night.'

Sonali looked at me, winked and smiled. How sensitively and intelligently she had handled the situation for her new Punjabi friend.

She was like a shield from then on, very protective. If any of the guys would try flirting with me, she would reprimand them. She was like a tigress, putting her point of view strongly and assertively, and no one dared to mess with her.

One morning, we were at the beach for horse-riding lessons. I just loved galloping away, and had always enjoyed this particular class. That day, a new white horse was assigned to me. Sonali didn't come for that particular class. I patted Toofan (I still remember his name) and galloped away. My teacher was happy that I was learning well. When I returned after a good ride, as I was getting off, with one foot still on the saddle, Toofan decided to run again. Suddenly, I was in mid-air with the horse running, and when I broke away, his speed flung me high in the air and I landed on the ground on my wrist.

Everything seemed to have slowed down. I was losing consciousness. My arm didn't feel like a part of me at all. I could see the others running towards me, shouting for help. My eyes were shutting. All I remember was mumbling one name with great difficulty. 'Sonali.'

When I opened my eyes, she was right next to me. I had multiple fractures in my right wrist, and needed a minor surgery and plaster. However, I was strangely very calm. I could see from the little window of the operation theatre, that this lovely girl was trying to peep in. She had a smile on her face, putting up a brave front. But I didn't miss that little tear she tried to hide.

Most of my classes came to a halt since I was incapacitated. Horse riding, of course. Swimming, dancing was allowed partially, where I was using only my left hand. But it was tough. I didn't know how to do things with my left hand—no writing, eating, or bathing. I felt lost again.

And then, she just took over. Right from feeding me, giving me medicines, helping me change, everything! She taught me how to write with my left hand. My dance performance in our class was a rocking hit thanks to her! I was dancing with the cast still on (that had many sweet messages written for me), and she had dressed me up for my performance making sure I looked my best. She would take me for long walks and chat with me when she saw me upset for missing out on so many fun classes. In solidarity, she would miss one or two too. I knew when she was around, I was good.

Our permanent adda was this chai stall outside the bungalow. All seven of us used to sit there and discuss our future, wondering how it would be when we finally ventured into the world outside, and how we would be received. There was fear of uncertainty and rejection too. But there was more hope and stars in our eyes. We used to lay bets on who would rock in the movies instantly. Sonali won hands down. She was star material, undoubtedly!

One day, there was a shooting happening in the bungalow next door, with Aamir and Salman, for *Andaz Apna Apna*. I climbed up the wall (in spite of my cast) to get a sneak peek at the heart-throbs. I was so excited to catch a glimpse of them. Then I gestured to Sonali to join in, but she stood there. With a confident smile and a lovely heroine pose she said, '*Dekhenge nahin, hum seedha kaam karenge inke saath!* (We will not watch, we will work with them straight away!)' We both did exactly that later. She with both Aamir and Salman, and I with Salman.

After we completed our course, everyone went their separate ways but Sonali and I stayed in touch.

Visiting each other's houses was a ritual. Her parents were simple and absolutely lovely people, and I still remember the number of tasty Maharashtrian lunches I have had with them. When we sat together or had stayovers at each other's homes, we would discuss our experiences in the industry. We both came from protected backgrounds. I was vulnerable and apprehensive but she was clear and confident, and a fighter. She inspired me.

Our prophecy had come true. She had signed the maximum number of movies, and was doing supremely well.

Later, she shifted her retired parents close to where she lived after she got married. Everything that she had aspired to do, she had made it happen with sheer willpower and strength of mind. It wasn't easy for her, with no filmi background, to establish herself. But in no time, she had taken to the industry like a fish to water; signing on the best of movies and becoming a sensation. I felt so proud to say that she was my friend. I was, on the other hand, making slow progress, more a part of multi-starrers than solo leads. The going was tough. Gradually, we both found our foothold and our journeys.

Years passed by. We weren't in touch as much, but whenever we met, it was like the good old times. And then, I invited her for my book launch, to read a chapter. She had met Ma, she was an integral part of my journey, and hence, I really wanted her to be there. Sonali smiled warmly when I went to invite her. 'Of course, I'm coming. First, you tell me how are you and why haven't you found a guy?' She was protective again.

Before I got this baffling news about her, the last time we spoke was when she had called. '*Aise hi kiya phone!* (Just called!) Come and meet. Lots to chat.'

And then came the disturbing news of her illness. Life is strange. We think everyone is as we last spoke to them (when I last spoke to her, she was absolutely fine, was my first thought). But life passes by. In no time, when we are busy with the everyday bhag-daud, running around, one fine day, a health scare just stops it all. I was shocked. A healthy, happy Sonali with no symptoms, was diagnosed with cancer. I felt terrible. I couldn't meet her as she was far away in New York for her treatment.

I went into flashback mode. It just felt like yesterday when she had looked after me while I was unwell, and now she was far, far away. I would see the pictures that she would post, reflecting that familiar strength of hers and that positive smile.

I knew she would overcome it too, like all her other battles. She hadn't gotten it easy ever, but she had won eventually, as always. This too would pass. It had to.

When she returned, I gave her a call. '*Milne aaun?* (Should I come and meet?) Loads to chat.'

I heard a girly giggle. *Aaja!* (Come!) The woman I met now was the same—a stunner—the charming one with a smile and the familiar glint in her eyes, who had taken life in her stride, faced it and fought it head-on.

However, there was an added maturity, of having understood life and pain a little more.

'*Kya legi*? Coffee? Did you find a guy?' We laughed, we giggled, we reminisced, we shared our pains, our joys, a few tears and lots of laughter!

Attagirl! You are a story to be told, a person who has inspired millions with her sheer grit, who made friends with life every time it threw challenges, in fact, challenging life itself.

Today too, I feel like you are the fairy I thought you were when I first met you, but one who made her own fairy tale. A beautiful one at that.

After all, you are the loveliest of them all.

JAVED AKHTAR

Jidhar jate hain sab udhar jana accha nahin lagta;
Mujhe paamal raaston ka safar accha nahin lagta!
(I don't like to tread on the oft beaten path)

His own words aptly describe him the best.

If I am ever asked who it is I admire and adore the most, it would be Javed saab. Whenever I talk to him, I feel that life is how you see it . . . and, in this case, it is bright, happy and full of celebrations. Because that's how it is when it is with Javed Akhtar.

I don't recollect when I first met him because I feel I have known him for ever. I had met him at get-togethers or events, but our interactions were always very formal. I had, of course, grown up on all the films he had written and hummed all the beautiful songs he had penned, but I wasn't sure whether he knew me well or if he just found my face familiar when we exchanged pleasantries. It was thanks to Shabana Azmi that I had the pleasure of knowing Javed saab well. It was at their Holi celebrations where I was first properly introduced to him by Shabana ji. And what an introduction it was! I was overwhelmed when she told him, 'Jaadu . . . (that's what she fondly calls him) . . . She's one of the finest we have.' He smiled and added, '*Bhai, Shabana keh rahi hain to zaroor koi baat hogi* (If Shabana says so, there must be something special about you).' And he welcomed me home.

That's how it has been for so many years now with my most favourite couple. Their place has been home for me and they've always made sure that I felt like family.

I remember I was leaving a film director's office after a meeting and saw Javed saab's name flash on my mobile. When I picked the call, I heard his distinct voice say, '*Accha suniye, apne dheron fans ki fehrist mein, sabse upar naam mera likh lein* (in the list of your numerous fans, please put my name on top).'

I barely managed to say bye to the director who had come to see me off and ran to the stairs to get to a quiet place and hear what Javed saab was saying. '*Bhai, abhi* Bhaag Milkha Bhaag *dekh kar aaye* . . . (We just saw *Bhaag Milkha Bhaag*). *Aisa kamaal kaise kar leti hain?* (How do you manage to create this magic?)'

I had tears in my eyes. *The* Javed Akhtar was telling me that! He was describing each moment he'd liked in detail. He was Farhan's father too, but he was generously complimenting another actor. It reflected his large-heartedness and the true creative person that he is. The phone was then passed on to Shabana ji who warmly and excitedly shared how much she loved the film, and both Farhan and me in it. I was bowing down; hands folded on my chest, standing alone on that staircase, in gratitude and reverence for them. They didn't need to, but they had made sure that they voiced their appreciation for another artist and made her day!

I ran home to Ma. I couldn't wait to tell her that Javed saab and Shabana ji had called me. She said, 'Great, beta. I am so happy! Then, after a pause, she added, 'How beautifully he writes, *hai na*?' She didn't say much but I knew that she was very touched that one of her favourite writers had called to compliment her daughter. She wrote a poem that night, dedicated to him. Much later, on one of Javed saab's birthdays, we framed that poem and gifted it to him. I can't express how beautiful it felt to see him graciously accept the heartfelt words that Ma had written for him.

Once, I had specially gone to Shabana ji's annual celebration on Kaifi saab's birthday, where several poets—new poets and veterans—were reciting their work. Javed saab was the last one to come up on stage. And when he did, he just took over! His hard-hitting lines and the way he recited them, infused so much vigour and energy in everyone around. We all straightened up to be able to grasp each word. The atmosphere at Janki Kutir had to be seen to be believed. There was a huge applause with requests for more recitals! No one wanted Javed saab to get off stage. His thoughts were revolutionary—liberal and deep— and they brought thoughts that were hidden deep inside to the fore, through the sheer magic of his words and the passionate manner in which they were recited.

After the session, when I met him to tell him how deeply impacted I was; he took me by surprise with a witty remark, completely in contrast to his mood from a few minutes ago. That day, I realized that I was talking to the wittiest man I had ever met. His one-liners had everyone in splits and he said them with a straight face, which made them even funnier.

Javed saab has this endearing quality of throwing in a deep-meaning thought between his jokes. It's for you to grasp it before he moves on to the next topic. I don't think I have ever enjoyed hearing anecdotes as much as when they are narrated by Javed saab! And this is because of three things; his range of experiences, his amazing memory—recollecting each incident the way it was—and the mischief and joy with which he narrates it, adding his personal touch. You have no choice but to listen to him, absolutely glued and mesmerized. He is undoubtedly the *jaan* of any get-together! One of the most learned men I know.

I feel so much joy to just listen to Javed saab talk about various topics and on life's philosophies too. I come back home a little more enlightened, a little happier that I was in such esteemed company. What I also love about him is that even if there has been a setback and you happen to discuss that with him, he brushes it off by joking about it instead. This amazes me no end. Nowadays, when people live and thrive on discussing their issues, this person faces them all with a dash of humour. Isn't that a blessing? You learn to befriend life this way, taking it as it comes and enjoying what it has to offer.

I have loved the bond he and Shabana ji share—that of friendship, which, in his own words, even marriage couldn't destroy. I have seen them pull each other up, pamper each other and be each other's best companions. They are my ideal couple.

It was heartwarming to see how Shabana ji celebrated her Jaadu's seventy-fifth birthday. From the Bollywood-themed party, where Javed saab was participating just as exuberantly in a polka-dotted outfit that matched Shabana ji's, to a chat session where he answered all questions posed to him with so much wit and sensitivity. I'll never forget when he said, 'It is so strange that when you start feeling that you have started understanding life, age has passed by. So, one should have a longer lifespan to enjoy life to the fullest!' I couldn't agree more. I cheered for this man who had celebrated each day of his life with elan, and lived each moment to the fullest.

When Shabana ji met with an accident, I ran to the hospital, where only very close relatives were allowed to go up to where she was. I went to visit too but I stood away from the family, to give them their privacy. Anyway, I was too shaken up to move. Javed saab looked in control of his emotions though I could feel a storm brewing inside him. He saw me in the corner, standing by myself and noticed what no one else had. He could see that I was devastated and awkward. He gestured to me to come and sit next to him. There was the warmth of a protective elder who spoke a lot with his silence. I felt a bit calmer and grateful that he had understood. Even in that critical situation, he was sensitive enough to observe.

During the lockdown, the first poem I had penned had gone viral. It was titled, *'Jab Sab Theek Hoga Na Toh Yeh Toh Karate Rahenge* (When everything becomes okay, we will continue to do this).' The very next day, I got a video call from Shabana ji. In her patent style, she started the conversation by pulling Javed saab's leg and said that he hadn't noticed the mole on her lips even after thirty-six years of marriage. And then Javed saab said, *'Bhai, inki aankhon se nazar hate toh kuch aur dekhen* (If only I can move my eyes past hers . . . only then will I be able to see something else).' The heaviness of the lockdown suddenly dissipated on seeing this lovely couple with such happy, smiling faces. Life felt so cheerful with them around. Suddenly, Shabana ji praised my poem and warmly said, *'Bahut achche* (very good).' And then, Javed saab took the phone and said, *'Bhai, main tumhara sabse bada fan hun. Bahut sunder likha . . . balki aur likho* (I'm your biggest fan. You wrote beautifully . . . Write more). I'll publish all your poems.'

When they hung up, I was crying. I was vulnerable in the lockdown anyway, with plenty of mood swings. Their warmth and affection and their belief in me overwhelmed me even more. Javed saab's words kept ringing in my ears and I just felt truly blessed. Javed Akhtar saying this to me was no small feat! It was surely a big deal.

They had shifted to their Khandala bungalow during the lockdown. It is aptly called Sukoon. I had major withdrawal symptoms due to not having seen them for a long time and as soon as the lockdown was relaxed, I visited them for lunch. To see the entire family together was a pleasure. We chatted, joked and listened to Javed saab's anecdotes. Oh, I had missed them so much! We played dumb charades and also had some serious discussions on the current scenario. Then, we had the most delicious meal together.

When it was time to leave, Javed saab thought of something, held my hand and took me out. Like a protective elder, he said, 'You are a very sensitive woman. So, make sure that whoever you find knows how to nurture it.' It is the kind of advice that probably only my parents would have given me. Shabana ji joined in too and told him about my disasters with relationships. Before it got serious, he changed it all with a joke, and we all cracked up as we said our goodbyes. How much love and warmth had I received from them! And I know that they have tried to fill the vacuum I have felt after Ma with all their hearts.

Recently, I called up Javed saab to congratulate him on being the first Indian to receive the prestigious Richard Dawkins Award for his courageous public stand on behalf of atheism and free thought. Who else could have been more deserving than he? He barely spoke about the award and started talking about my work instead! What humility! I was stumped yet again.

One day, I was sitting and writing something when I got a call from Javed saab. '*Bhai, tumhara ek Cadbury ad dekha* (saw a Cadbury ad of yours). We were six people sitting in the room. Tanvi Azmi, Baba, a few others and me. We all are of the opinion that you are a terrific actor.' And then one by one, all of them congratulated me. I was left speechless. There may be many people who may admire you but how many of them actually take the effort to pick up the phone and let you know? That call brought a priceless, huge smile on my face!

Javed saab, you are truly special. I have been inspired by your writing, your poetry and your grit and strength to face life head-on. As you say, 'Kya darein zindagi mei kya hoga, kuch na hoga toh tajurba hoga (Why should we be afraid of what will happen in life? If nothing else, it will be an experience).' I am trying to inculcate that fearlessness in me.

With your wit and humour, I have experienced some of the happiest moments with you that I shall carry in my bag of memories forever. From your immense knowledge, I have learnt a lot and have become so inclined to your world of poetic words. With your affection and warmth, I feel more enriched and with your compliments, I tend to better myself every time.

I have observed you closely Javed saab—as a husband, a father, a poet-writer, a friend, philosopher and guide, a free thinker and speaker—and I find myself falling short of words to tell you how I feel.

I can only quote Ma's words from her poem for you: 'Tum to itna accha likh lete ho, khwabon ko hawaon se choo lete ho, mere lafzon mei kuch waisi hi siyahi bhar do . . . (You write so well, you touch dreams while riding the wind, fill my words with the same ink . . .)'

And I surely want to add, 'Aapke dheron fans ki lambi fehrist mein, sabse upar naam mera likh lein.'

NASEERUDDIN SHAH

Be it *Sparsh*, *Mirch Masala*, *Mandi*, *Masoom*, *Junoon* or any of his other films—I've been an ardent admirer of his acting since childhood. The little me was absolutely mesmerized when I watched him perform. His eyes spoke volumes. So, one day, I asked my mother, 'Ma what's his name? I love his acting!' She smiled. 'Me too! His name is Naseeruddin Shah!'

Now, I was intrigued with the name too!

While growing up, I wouldn't miss a single film of his, *Ijaazat* being my favourite, followed by *Katha*, *Mirza Ghalib*, and many others. And then I saw him dance to the tune of '*Tirchi Topi Wale . . .*', I was floored. Was there a role Naseeruddin Shah could not do? And that too so well! If ever by a twist of fate, I became an actor, I would love to perform that kind of a variety, I would often think to myself.

I couldn't have even imagined then that years later I would actually be in the movies and my third film, *Daava*, would be opposite him! The 1990s were the *daur* of masala multi-starrers, and this one had Akshay Kumar and Raveena Tandon. To say that I was over the moon to be in the same frame as Naseeruddin Shah as his love interest was an understatement.

I was a giggly teenager trying to act mature in front of the man I absolutely looked up to. Of course, his eyes observed everything. There was an amused look that appeared for a bit and then disappeared. Then he was into the scene!

I was most excited about doing a sensual romantic number with him—the characteristic filmi rain song! My fantasy of doing a typical heroine number was finally coming true, and that too with Naseeruddin Shah! But I couldn't say the same for him. He didn't look very comfortable doing it but he didn't say anything.

Years passed by and my interactions with him would be when I'd go to watch his plays at Prithvi Theatre and meet him backstage. He's an enigma on stage too and so passionate about theatre. His performances on stage also leave you awestruck. Be it the biggest monologues or the silent moments, the ease, intensity and level of involvement with which they are performed, give you goosebumps! Post the shows, I would go to just wish and congratulate him. During those quick chats what would surprise me were his references to some of my performances. I felt lucky that he had been following my work and that he thought I was doing some noticeable stuff. And he would always remember to mention that rain song. 'O god, the song sequence we did was so awkward for me . . . that too with a little girl!' I'd immediately add, '. . . but I thoroughly enjoyed it!' and we'd both laugh about it.

Finally, I got the opportunity to work with him again in a film called *Irada*, which incidentally also got me my first National Award. I didn't have many scenes with him but nevertheless, I was supremely excited about them. We also got some time to sit and chat between shots. I observed that he was very transparent with his moods. If he found that something was disorganized or not up to the mark on the sets, he would show his displeasure. And if he cracked one-liners and made witty remarks, it was a given that he was enjoying being on set. I loved his sense of humour—subtle and sharp—yes, both, if you caught it!

For me, the most precious time spent with him was when I had gone to his house to gift him my book, *Me and Ma*. He was kind enough to invite me home for a cup of chai. I loved his house and the way he and his lovely wife, Ratna Pathak Shah, had done it up: simple, classy and airy! The conversation that ensued that day had me adore him a little more, be in awe of him a little more and, of course, enlightened a little more too, with the immense knowledge that he has about anything under the sun. He spoke about his love for theatre and the new play that he was working on. What I completely loved was his straightforward honesty—of calling a spade a spade. No mincing words!

I met him again after a few months at Prithvi and I went up to him to say hi. He whispered in my ears, 'I saw another good performance of yours . . . in a not-so-good film,' he added with a naughty grin. It brought an instant smile to my face. Yes, I absolutely adore him!

I remember an occasion when I needed his advice. As much as I am apprehensive about calling someone up, I felt that I had to talk to him that day. In fact, I felt completely at ease just picking up the phone and speaking with him. And I am glad I did. What I got from him was not only sound advice but also words of reassurance. As I hung up, my heart was filled with the warmth that he had exuded.

The most heartwarming memory of him is having received the sweetest ever message from him after I won the National Award. I read it once, and then again. I smiled and then I had tears—some moments can't be expressed in words. This was one of them.

Naseer saab, you are truly a gem, someone I am extremely fond of. Also, there is something I will never be able to tell you in person. I've always wished for a guy who exudes the romance you did when you held Shabana ji's pallu and sang, 'Huzoor iss kadar bhi na itra ke chaliye . . .' in Masoom. *That love and masti in the eyes! No one has even come close.*

But then the standards set by you will always be too high to achieve, hai na?

RAJU HIRANI

'*Jaadu ki jhappi*' has now become a household mantra. It showed the power of a simple warm hug which probably wouldn't take away the loneliness, the pain or suffering—but it surely gave the person receiving it the solace and strength to move on with a smile.

Be it *Munnabhai M.B.B.S.*, *Lage Raho Munna Bhai* or *3 Idiots*, or any other film of his, Raj Kumar Hirani or Raju Hirani as he is fondly called, has given audiences some much-needed cheer. Big smiles and the goodness that spilled over from his movies have made people feel that 'all is well'.

Yes, he has the audience eating out of his hands. They love his movies, and feel as if it's their story he's telling; find the protagonist completely relatable, cry and laugh with him which leaves them wanting more! And that is the magic of his movies!

I did one of my first ads with him for a detergent. I was fairly new in the business then. As I set my foot on the set, I was pleasantly surprised to see a very happy atmosphere all around. Of course, there was a lot of hustle and bustle, but no one looked stressed or hyper. They were all happily going about their business. And it had to be the captain of the ship who exuded that positivity that I was experiencing all around. I was finally introduced to him. Simple, a bit shy and extremely soft-spoken, he said his pleasantries and started explaining the shot.

After all my close shots, came a very technical shot. I had to bring the product at a specific point close to the camera (not a centimetre here or there as focus on the product would be lost). I am, to be honest, very technically challenged. So, while all my close shots had been done in one or two takes, this shot was taking for ever. I was feeling pathetic for not being able to deliver. With each passing shot, my hand was shaking with nervousness. Then I saw Raju ji walking towards me. I thought I would surely get a scolding. Instead, he laughed. 'It happens with everyone, don't bother. Just relax and do it in reverse order. Bring the pack to the focal point first and then measure it backwards . . . bas . . . simple.' His smile put me at ease. The world had not ended yet!

I did as I was told and this time, I was smiling too. Yes, the shot was taken immediately. And that man sitting next to the monitor gave me a thumbs up. I wish I had half the calmness he possessed but a little had surely rubbed off on me that day. I did realize that things work out a lot better if done with a calm frame of mind.

That ad went on to become a big hit and I, a popular face in the world of advertisements.

A few years later, I was at Ramoji Film City in Hyderabad when I got a call from him. Pleasantly surprised, I instantly picked it up. 'Hi Divya, Raju here . . . *kaisi ho? . . . kahan ho?* (how are you? . . . where are you?)' I had the brightest smile on my face as I spoke to him, I told him that I was in Hyderabad and would be back in two days. He came straight to the point. '*Accha* . . . I am making *Munnabhai M.B.B.S.* and I want you to do a song for me, can you come back and meet me please.'

'Of course, I would love to sir! What is it?'

'*Aa jao . . . phir batata hun* (Come back, then we will talk about it at length).'

Sure enough, as soon as I set foot in Mumbai, I fixed up a meeting with him. On the very next day, I was sitting with him having a delicious adrak chai. We exchanged pleasantries, and that shy smile was still intact. '*Accha . . .* the thing is, in the film, the hero, Sanjay Dutt, comes to meet his dying friend (Jimmy Sheirgill) in the hospital and promises to fulfil his last wish of feeling the love he had missed out in his life. So, I need an actor who can portray all emotions of love just with her eyes. She sits next to him and makes him feel all the love, while singing that song to him. It's a slow, sweet number like yesteryear movies and I want Pradeep Sarkar (the ace ad/filmmaker) to choreograph it.'

I was mesmerized. I would absolutely love to do this as an actor! It was challenging and inspiring at the same time. I was beaming and before I could utter a word, he said, '*Chalo phir.*'

'Where?' I asked, surprised.

'Let's go and meet Pradeep Sarkar,' he said. 'I will introduce you to him and discuss the concept in detail.'

This was truly amazing!

In no time, we reached Pradeep da's office.

I was extremely elated to be sitting with two brilliant directors together, who were explaining the song situation to me. We had a lovely meeting and by the end of it, I was a super excited actor waiting to perform on this song.

A few days later though, I got a call from Raju ji, with the same warm and affectionate voice, but a slight hesitation in it.

'Divya, sorry *yaar*, we had to change the concept of the song and it is now a proper dance number. I was so excited to work with you but this one is not working out.' Of course, I was a bit heartbroken, but I loved the grace and genuineness with which he had picked up the phone and honestly told me how it was. The song, *'Dekh Le'* became a huge hit.

Not that I lost out at all! In fact, I worked on several ads with Pradeep Sarkar post our meeting and gained a very dear friend for life—Raju Hirani.

That last phone call had somewhere created a beautiful bond of understanding between us. The sensitivity I had felt had struck a chord. I think it also reflects in his movies and that is why he is the man with the Midas touch. All his movies are well-loved and have gone on to become huge hits. Our tête-à-têtes on life and its myriad facets continued and I would often take back deep insights from these conversations.

I will always remember that beautiful Diwali evening at his house where, knowing my love for poetry and liking how I recite it, he made me recite a few poems amidst loud cheers. After that, Boman Irani played his guitar and sang, *'Give me some sunshine, give me some rain . . .'* in a mesmerizing manner! All of us joined in with him in unison. It was the same overwhelming feeling of goodness, positivity and elation that I see in his movies as well—it leaves one with a warm and festive feeling, with everyone genuinely enjoying themselves.

Another precious memory etched in my mind is that of a phone call to him when I was going through a very low phase emotionally (I had just broken-up). Not that I talk to Raju ji very often—maybe once in a few months—but that day, in my lowest moment, I could only think of calling this gentle human being. I just dialled the number of the 'All is well' director. I so needed to feel the same way!

To date, I don't know why I called him as I hadn't discussed any personal stuff with him ever, but my heart knew that talking to him would make me feel better.

As I heard 'Hi Divya', I couldn't utter a word. What would I say about why I had called? That I had broken-up and wanted to feel strong, positive and reassured, hearing his voice that was warmth personified itself? I couldn't fake a bright 'Hi' either. So, what just remained was silence. After a big pause, he asked, 'Are you okay?' I managed to say, *'Nahi, aise hi phone kia . . .* (I just called like that)' literally trying to stop myself from sobbing.

I heard the same calm voice from the other side, *'Divya, life hai yaar. Aaj achchi nahi hai toh kal better hogi* (It's life. If it's not good today, it will get better tomorrow), don't take it so seriously.' Then he added, 'I am in America, *aate hi milta hun . . .* (meet you when I'm back), cheer up.'

I realized that day that I love my world of films because it has people who have mastered their craft and are great human beings too! I derive a lot of happiness and inspiration from them. It fills me with pride and elation that I belong to the same world as them, sharing the same passion and the high that movie-making gives! Raju Hirani tops the list of those people and hence, speaking to him put me at peace in a very unassuming way that day. A heavy load seemed to have been lifted off my chest and a voice inside me reminded, 'All is well'.

Yes, we all have to walk our own paths and fight our own battles but sometimes, people who matter, especially those that we look up to, can just make that journey smoother.

Thank you, Raju ji, for being a huge moral support, always. With a friend like you, life is nothing short of being 'all well.' And yes, a big 'jaadu ki jhappi' to you!

ANUPAM KHER

He has been someone whose company I've enjoyed a lot. It's interesting to note that even when he makes light of every situation, he is a serious student of life. To me, Anupam Kher is someone whose mere presence exudes positivity. Whenever I meet him or talk to him, I feel '*sab badhiya hai*' (all is good) and life is full of hope and miracles.

We did some multi-starrers together and a film called *Morning Walk*. I remember he had been kind enough to drop me home once when my driver had not turned up at the shoot. And then, Ma had made her famous aloo ki tikkis for him. Both of them chatted as if they had known each other forever. He had treated Ma like a child, totally indulging her, and she had loved every bit of it.

I got to know him better during the shoot of *Special 26*. Akshay, he and I would play word games between shots. To be in the company of two of the most entertaining men in the industry was an absolute delight. They would both crack jokes, pull each other's leg and then give some amazing shots! Work was so much fun, laughter and masti with them. On the sets, I saw Anupam ji discussing his scenes very seriously with Neeraj Pandey, our director. I observed that he had a child-like exuberance to perform a particular shot again and after he did it, the happy glint in his eyes showed his passion for his work clearly. He seemed very happy about a shot well done and then he excitedly looked at Neeraj for his reaction. Watching him wait in anticipation for the director's response was endearing to say the least!

Many months later, I was a bit upset for not getting a film I was very keen on. I reached home pretty disappointed when Ma told me that we had been invited by Anupam ji to see his show, *Kuch Bhi Ho Sakta Hai*. Ma and I reached the venue pretty early, so I took her inside the empty auditorium to get her seated comfortably. What I didn't expect was to see Anupam ji already on the stage, rehearsing. He saw us from a distance and waved to us. We went down to have a chat and Ma was ecstatic after speaking to him. As we walked back to our seats, I wondered how he was in such a jovial mood just before a solo performance. Had I been in his place, I would have been crazy nervous! Before I had even completed this thought of mine, I heard him shout out to us, '*Taaliyan zorr se bajana, thoda nervous hun*! (Clap hard, I'm a bit nervous!)' Now I was even more surprised! An actor of his stature—with hundreds of movies and awards to his credit—was grounded enough to admit his true feelings without any hesitation.

In his play, he spoke, in a lighter vein, about all the crises that had taken place in his life. All that could go wrong had gone wrong but he had finally made it, despite it all. It takes a very secure man to laugh at himself and his mistakes and he owned up to them beautifully. And the audience showed their appreciation and owned him beautifully too after the play as he bowed down to thank everyone! He didn't use any well-rehearsed lines to express his gratitude to the audience—he was transparent, vulnerable and grateful. People loved his honesty and straightforward manner. When I left the auditorium, I also left behind my sadness over having lost a film. I was all set to face life head-on! Somehow, inside that auditorium, with his words; his play and with his performance, Anupam ji had given me renewed enthusiasm. If he could get up and walk after so many obstacles, and still believe in miracles, why was a single hurdle holding me back? I thanked him in my heart. The power of his words and performance and his life had motivated me big time.

All my meetings with him have left me smiling. Once, I had gone to his acting institute to take a master class for his students. He was waiting to chat with me over a cup of chai before he left. He is someone I feel extremely comfortable with to pour out my heart to, so in that half hour, I told him a few of my woes (we were meeting after a long time and there was a lot of catching up to do). He looked at me seriously. I had rarely seen this side of him. When he started talking, I kept looking at him in a daze. In front of me was a deep, intense man, who had seen so much in life that not only had he learnt to laugh at it but he had also learnt to make friends with life. When I asked him how, he quoted his grandfather's lines, '*Bheega hua aadmi baarish se nahi darta!* (A man who is already drenched does not fear the rain!)'

I wished I could keep listening to him but it was time for my master class. I was wondering what I would teach that day when I was just loving being a student myself of this amazing man.

I also relate to his love for his mother. It reminds me of my relationship with mine. I love the way he celebrates her! He introduced the world to his adorable, full-of-life mother, Dulari. He captures endearing conversations with her and posts them on social media. The way he pulls her leg and teases her, it feels as if he is still her little child. A person who's been a success, is truly inspiring, and is lauded by the whole world, is still his mother's little one! In a world where people grow up too soon and take themselves very seriously, how beautiful is that!

I also learnt another amazing thing from him—to leave voice notes rather than written texts. The first time I sent him a message when he was shooting in the US for his international series, I was pleasantly surprised to receive a voice note, and a very warm one at that. It left me smiling too! He had said, 'Voice notes are so much more personal and warm, *dost. Aur phir typing ki mehnat bhi nahi!* (No need to type!)' After that, I've always left voice notes for people I interact with.

Kher saab—I don't know when I started addressing you that way—but I love it! You are someone I will always hold very dear. You inspire and motivate me, and bring a big smile to my face. When I am low or vulnerable, I always remember what you say, 'Do the best you can in a tough situation and don't forget to befriend life and smile at the challenges it throws.'

It makes me happy, talking about you. After all, with you, I always feel, 'sab badhiya hai!'

RAJIT KAPUR

Rajit is someone whom I call my Santa Claus. And it's been a friendship of about twenty years that has gradually but surely got me to give him this very well-deserved title.

I, of course, knew the *Byomkesh Bakshi* star and of his award-winning performances in *The Making of the Mahatma* and *Suraj Ka Satvan Ghoda*, but I saw him for the first time on the sets of my second film, *Train to Pakistan*. He and I didn't share any screen space in that film, but we met during one of the schedules where I had joined and he was leaving in a day.

I had a night shoot, and I was told that I had to sing and dance myself. The saving grace was that it was a night shoot in the cold winters, and the unit wasn't expecting any spectators. But I was nervous. I hadn't tested my singing skills in front of a film unit ever, and I was petrified.

During lunch, I had bumped into Rajit, who was leaving the next day. He said hi to me, and I happened to utter my woes. He was laughing, and then said matter-of-factly, 'Why are you worrying? We'll all come to cheer you up. And don't think so much and stress yourself, just go with the flow.'

At night, with the musicians, I started to perform, trying my best to sing. Dancing, of course, I enjoyed, but I was tense. I saw Rajit from the corner of my eye. He was standing very far, so that he wouldn't be seen, but his eyes were focused on my performance. Suddenly, we heard a loud thud. Everyone wondered where the sound had come from.

In the darkness of the night, the light men turned their huge lights to the other side to see what had happened. To our utter disbelief, the entire village was sitting there, covered in their blankets to fight the cold. They had all come to see the dance, and from that crowd, one of those perched on a wall had fallen. I was shocked. There was sudden chaos.

Suddenly, a few villagers came to the set, and asked the assistant director innocently, 'When will she dance again?'

The simple-minded villagers thought it was a little function where a girl was dancing, and they surely didn't want to miss it. I was both amused and scared. Suddenly, I felt a hand pull me. It was Rajit. He pulled me inside, removed his shawl and wrapped me in it protectively. When the villagers were settled outside and had agreed to peacefully watch the performance and not cross the boundary line assigned to them, I was asked to come and give the shot.

This time, I knew I had a large audience. Holding my hand tight, Rajit brought me out and said, 'Don't bother about who and how many people are watching you. Perform for yourself. Go and have a blast on the stage. Break a leg!' This surely came from his theatre background—the discipline and the work ethic.

I was still unsure. He stood close to me, away from the camera, and cheered me up. Then, as if on cue, the entire unit and then the villagers started clapping too! The atmosphere had turned encouraging and it warmed me up. I danced and sang and I forgot who was in front of me. I was in a trance now, really enjoying and having a blast. The shot was cut with louder cheers, and this time, I ran to Rajit myself and held his hand. It made me feel secure, protected, and cared for. That became our equation on the sets of *Train to Pakistan*, and that's how it still is, twenty years later.

The next film wasn't too far apart from this one. I was signed up for Shyam Benegal's film *Samar*, and I was delighted to know that Rajit and Rajeshwari were in it too. *Samar* was being shot in a small town, Sagar, in MP. To my dismay, my hotel was away from where Rajit, Raj and Shyam babu were staying. It was a very small place and as I was the last one in the cast to join, there was no room (no pun intended). But the sensitive crew that they all were, they made sure I didn't miss out on good company. So, Rajit, Raj, Seema Biswas and Yashpal Sharma would come and pick me up and take me to the hotel they were staying in on free days, and then drop me back. I was the pampered one.

My birthday happened to come during that schedule, and Rajit and Rajeshwari went looking for a cake for me in that small town. Obviously, there was no bakery there. But they asked around quite a bit and finally someone guided the two to a small grocery store. When the owner was asked for a cake, he took one out, not from a fridge but a cupboard, and offered it with a statutory warning. 'This is a few days old but edible.' The two of them brought it on the set victoriously, and as Shyam babu and I tried to cut my so-called birthday cake together, nothing happened to the cake, but yes, the knife broke.

Birthday cake or not, it was one of the most fun days for me, and that's always been the case with Rajju, as he's fondly called. Never mind what the destination has been, the journey has been beautiful. Always.

Rajju's house in Madh Island has been the adda for all of us friends to meet there frequently. His house is surrounded by greenery and it overlooks the beach—a haven in Mumbai, far from the maddening crowd. What makes our visits special is not just the destination, but how he just takes charge of looking after and feeding each one of us. He's known to make his own salads, mixing everything healthy from his fridge, cooking up his own recipes, and serving them with a lot of love. Also, he gets a few things made for dinner, but before that, it's a ritual to have our chai sessions in the nearby resort, watching the sunset together and sneaking in some hot vada pavs at the beach and mischievously munching on them with our faces covered.

My mom used to love accompanying me to Rajju's house. Once, I was to go directly to his house after work, and she called him up to complain about me. 'Listen, this girl is not taking me along. Am I not your friend?' she asked in a child-like manner. Rajit and Ma had a very special bond. In fact, seeing Ma's love for the colour purple and the number of clothes she had in that colour, Rajju had fondly named her Purple.

Ma would share a lot with him—what worried her about me, what she wanted him to sort for me, etc. For her, he was the big boy in charge, who would never say no to Ma.

When Ma went away, he was the first man I called. He was there through my rough days; he sat with me to write and prepare a befitting tribute for her. In fact, on the day she left, he had come to visit and when he left, the song, *'Rahen naa rahen hum, mehakaa karenge'* (We may or may not live but we will be around like fragrance)', was playing in his car ominously. It was he who chose that very song for the tribute we put together for our Purple.

I told him, just like Ma used to say *haq se* (with confidence), 'Listen, you have to be there for my book launch, and be the master of ceremonies.' He, of course, was there throughout. And he spoke that day, with all his heart, about all the hues of his 'Purple'. No one would have been able to describe Ma like that.

Rajit is a very emotional person and extremely sensitive too, but what he also has, is an amazing quality to protect his sensitivity. He doesn't dwell on a situation for too long. He faces a situation, absorbs it, and lets it go by getting engrossed in something else that helps him get away from the situation. When he saw me totally indulging in my mess, he would spend time with me, and make me do things that distracted me from my depression. He would, in a matter-of-fact manner, tell me how to deal with it. In such matters, he's the strict and practical one, and I always follow his advice.

We have always been in touch. At his place, we would go to the beach for walks. It's another issue that given his fast pace, I could never keep up and ended up running to catch up.

Then, we worked a lot together. I would also go for most of his stage shows. I would look forward to him performing on stage, because he's a revelation on it; his passion and involvement is to be seen to be believed. On stage, he is exactly as he had told me to be too, during *Train to Pakistan*. He's a different man there, performing with so much passion and energy, that I wonder how he does it—always a new avatar and a new aspect of Rajit Kapur. After every show, being in the audience and giving him a standing ovation fills me with an immense sense of pride for being his friend.

My New Year celebrations have been mostly with him and our group. He makes amazing plans that are in far-off wilderness or jungles, where he disconnects himself from the world for that one week. I usually join in for two–three days, but even in those few days, I feel amply rejuvenated to take on the world. With Rajju, when you travel, you really don't have to bother much. He takes charge completely, from planning everything including travel, stay, food, plans for the day and everything else. With him, I have enjoyed and discovered nature at close quarters.

He loves trying everything new possible in a given place. So, in one day, you can expect him to plan two jungle safaris, tea at a famous hilltop close by and whatever adventure sport activity is available around too! But the standard and loveliest part of the plan is to always begin the New Year early in the morning, with a visit to the local temple, and watch the first sunrise of the New Year together. That experience, with all friends together, is surreal and divine. He makes sure we experience the best in a given place, and totally juice up the time we have together.

I remember our trip to Coonoor during one such New Year. While we had gone shopping to pick up local stuff, we came upon a local rice wine. None of us tried it, but Rajju, the experimental guy that he is, had to try it out for the novelty. So, he tasted it, and fell ill. We all thought that the New Year wouldn't go well with him in bed. All plans would go awry. But Rajju made sure our plans didn't change.

Rajju doesn't take medication. He builds his immunity with naturopathy. So, he sat in the room, taking care of his health, not allowing us to pamper him too much. With his sheer grit, determination, and good diet, he was up and about in no time! On New Year's Eve too, he was all ready and fresh. I was amazed at his willpower.

He had told us to gather at a designated place. We all dressed up and reached that spot, specially booked by Rajit. We lit a little bonfire and then Rajju gave us all New Year's gifts that he had meticulously packed for each one of us. Then, he asked us to narrate an incident each that had changed our lives for the better. Initially, everyone was inhibited, but when one of us started narrating, and then the other, the energy there changed—there was positivity, there was hope, and there was love and unity in just honestly baring our hearts out to each other. And finally, we all held hands and prayed for a lovely New Year! The most peaceful and beautiful way to ring in the New Year—the Rajit Kapur way. It was, of course, followed by the annual ritual of waking up early to see the sunrise together from a temple.

He is the reason that despite our busy schedules, we manage to catch up regularly. Rajit is a workaholic, with everything meticulously planned, from stage shows and rehearsals, to shoots and meetings. Yes, no breather. So, to fix a time to meet is always a tough task, but I must say, he always finds a way and the time to meet the people he cares for. Even if we have a bit of time, he'll quickly come with a gift or some food, have a cup of tea, give a big hug and run off.

In the crazy, busy lives we lead, I have never seen Rajju let life pass by when we were busy doing other things. He enjoys every scenario life throws at him and relishes and absorbs everything.

Well, Rajju, I have learnt to enjoy the now and the present to the best of my ability, thanks to you. I have also learnt that life is all about the moments you make and cherish.

This is just to say that I adore you, Rajit Kapur, for happening in my life, for wrapping that shawl around me protectively even now, for holding my hand tight, and yes, for walking briskly ahead of me, only to lovingly stop and look behind with laughter; waiting for me to catch up, and holding your friend's hand again. Tight.

Well, life sure is a party with you in it, my Santa.

ANUBHAV SINHA

'Aapki baat kaise taal dein? Aap buzurg hain hamare! (How can I not listen to you? You are, after all, my respected elder!)'

Even though he's older, he often calls me his 'buzurg' (elder). I truly love it because then I get to tell him that in that case, he must listen to me! That's the equation we have and I absolutely adore him for pulling my leg.

It is not often that one comes across a combination of traits that I see in Anubhav Sinha—so intelligent, well-read and with his own strong individual opinions, yet so happy-go-lucky. Almost a child at heart. And yes, a complete foodie!

Of course, I had known him for his blockbuster commercial films. But he amazed everyone by deciding to change his path one fine day—he shifted to making movies on hard-hitting issues and they have been so impactful. The first among them was *Mulk,* an absolutely thought-provoking film which got the nation thinking and shook everyone!

One fine day, I received a call from someone in his office stating that Anubhav Sinha wanted to talk to me. I had never met him before, so there was a second's hesitation before I spoke to him on the phone. I was immediately drawn in. He was completely at ease while talking; there was a comfort and apnapan to this tone, as if he had known me for long. That eased me up too. '*Bhai, suno . . . actually main ek film bana raha hun* (Hey listen, I'm making a film) . . . and you will be the last one to be cast, if you say yes. I'll be honest, you are an obvious choice for that role. Everyone told me to take you for this role and that is why I was doubtful *ki obvious choice lagega, but nahin yaar, tum hi karo film!* (never mind, you do the film!) *Script bhej raha hun . . . achi lage, to ajao yaar set pe jaldi!* (I'm sending you the script. If you like it, come to the set soon!)'

By the time I hung up, it felt like I had known him forever! He has a warm and affectionate way with people—he makes them his own.

I read the script and had a hearty laugh! I thoroughly enjoyed the witty script and loved my role! I told my manager to fit this film in my schedule somehow. Thankfully, everyone I was working with was kind enough to adjust and I reached Lucknow. On the sets of my first Anubhav Sinha film!

The cast of this film included the best actors in business— Pankaj Tripathi, Saurabh Shukla, Richa Chadha, Vinay Pathak, Pavan Malhotra and Kumud Mishra. Since I was the last one to join the gang, I hadn't discussed the role with Anubhav Sinha at all. So, when I excitedly asked him, 'Sir, should I take up this mannerism for my role?' He promptly replied, 'Oh, Saurabh is doing that.' I sighed and then came up with another idea but he said, 'Err, Richa is doing that . . .' By the end of it, I was done with all ideas and sulking, '*. . . ab phir main kya karun?* (now what should I do?)' Since the film was a whacky satire, everyone had distinct mannerisms in the film. And every mannerism that occurred to me was already sold out! Anubhav saw my crestfallen face and understood. Both of us sat on the cement parapet outside the hotel lobby, chewing on Lucknowi paan. I was chewing slowly since I was also sulking.

He was silent for a while, chewing thoughtfully. As he finished his paan he said, '*Kal batata hun kuch accha sa tumhare liye. Tension mat le* (I will tell you something tomorrow, don't get tensed).'

The shoot was scheduled for the next day and I didn't know what my approach to my role was! I was nervous. Everyone else had their stuff prepared and I felt like such a late entrant. But his words had given me solace. There's something about him that makes you put all your trust in him.

I reached the set and saw Pankaj and Saurabh performing. I stood amazed, but honestly, that also made me more nervous and conscious about my unpreparedness! I greeted Anubhav Sinha and he responded pleasantly. I was waiting for him to give me a brief but he didn't seem to remember at all! He was engrossed in the shots he was taking and rightly so. I seated myself right in front of him and kept looking at him at intervals to remind him that I was tense but he didn't look at me at all. 'Well, I think I'll be sulking on this set despite the fact that all my actor friends are here,' I thought.

As the scene got over and I had almost given up, he looked at me straight. '*Aao dost, thoda batiya lein* (Come my friend, let's chat).' So he hadn't forgotten after all!

We went out in the open, and sat outside in the fresh air. There was silence as he sipped his tea. I was waiting rather nervously and then he spoke. He gave me such an interesting perspective on the role that it totally bowled me over! Yes . . . I was sitting with a very sensitive director who had a very nuanced approach to everything but almost always laughed it off as nothing!

Now I was back in business on the set, fully clear about what I was to do!

His sets are a joy even when you are doing a serious scene. The atmosphere was so light! He would deliver funny one-liners after a good shot, and most definitely did not miss opportunities to pull my leg. He would then treat us all to the most amazing delicacies that he'd order from special food joints he knew of. By the end of the shoot, I almost felt like I did not want to go back home. The shoot was like a picnic where I had also worked and rather well at that. All thanks to Anubhav Sinha, we all had a blast as actors and as friends.

This bond with him continued post the shoot of that film too over a few awesome food sessions discussions on subjects we felt strongly about like poetry, books, scripts and of course, it never ended without the ritualistic leg pulling and laughter!

He made some beautiful films recently—*Article 15* and *Thappad*—both issue-based, that were bold, sensitive and very hard-hitting. I was so amazed at how he was choosing his subjects and saying what he had to so beautifully. When he was making *Thappad*, he called me up and said, 'Hello Lambu!' I laughed. We chatted and joked for a while and then he said, '*Yaar, film bana raha hun . . . Thappad . . .* six actresses *hain par tum nai ho. Maine socha bata dun!* (I'm making a film, there are six actresses in it but you are not one of them. Thought I'd let you know!)' I was so touched by his sensitivity. He didn't have to tell me that, but I loved his straightforwardness and his concern about how I would feel not being a part of it. I mustered, 'You decided so it must be the right decision . . .' He told me the story in brief; spoke about the cast and then said, '*Shoot kar ke aata hun phir milte hain* . . . (Let me shoot and come back and then let's meet).'

I ended up meeting him at the premiere of *Thappad*. As I stood on the red carpet outside the theatre posing for the shutterbugs, he came from behind and hugged me. '*Achchi film banayi hai, Lambu!* (I've made a good film, tall one!)' He was beaming and when I got out after watching the film, I was beaming too, with pride. I could see a director who had the hunger to tell stories—stories that needed to be told—stories that he was telling with panache!

Post the lockdown, he was amongst the first people I met. I was missing getting my leg pulled and all the laughter. He specially ordered a delicious meal for me and we chatted over a yummy lunch. I said, '*Aaj khichayi hi nahi hui!* So how will I become taller if you don't pull my leg?'

He smiled. '*Madam aisa hai . . . ki aap jitney zameen ke bahar hain, utni hi andar bhi hain* (You are as much under the ground as above) . . . *depth hai!*'

I was surprised. He had said this for the first time. I knew then that he noticed and observed everything. In his characteristic style, he then changed the topic with one of his witty one-liners.

Toh yun hai, Anubhav sir (So the thing is, Anubhav sir) that I am very enriched to have known you in my journey; to have shared laughter with you and some tears, and to have been directed by you.

I am waiting for my discussions with you on the parapets of every possible place, feeling the fresh air, and yes, chewing on a paan in absolutely great company!

DEV ANAND

Who could possibly be more good looking than him, when he hummed, '*Main zindagi ka saath nibhata chala gaya* . . . (I moved along in the direction life took me).' And what better way to describe him than with these amazing lines!

Dev Anand, the evergreen star with a penchant for life that is unparalleled! I have been super fortunate to have known him and worked with him.

He was among the first stars who I had met when I was doing the rounds of the industry. The euphoria of meeting the legend was inexplicable! I went to his office and was ushered into his cabin. I was a rank newcomer then, with no films and no references. He had still been kind enough to meet me when I had requested an appointment. When I entered his office, I heard a very familiar voice welcoming me in. There he sat—Dev Anand—well-dressed, just like in his films and absolutely stylish! It took me a few minutes to gather my nerves and digest the fact that I was actually in a meeting with Dev Anand. He was very warm and promised to call me if there was something for me in his films.

He kept his word. A few years later, I got a call. The voice was distinctly his but he still introduced himself in his patent style. He said, '*Divya, Dev bol raha hun. Ek film bana raha hun aur tumhare liye ek sunder role hai, office aa paogi?* (I'm making a film and there is a beautiful role for you. Will you be able to come to the office?)'

I was enamoured with the charming way in which he offered me the role. Who could have ever refused this charismatic star? And to work with him would be an experience I knew I'd cherish all my life. I instantly said yes.

I was to play Dev saab's daughter-in-law, a big star who's always at loggerheads with him. The film was *Chargesheet* and also had Naseeruddin Shah and Jackie Shroff (both of them ardent admirers of Dev Anand). We were to shoot in the picturesque hill town of Mahabaleshwar and Ma had accompanied me to the shoot. On the first day, as Ma and me were having our morning tea, we heard a knock at the door. Wondering who had come in the morning, Ma opened the door. She froze on seeing Dev saab. He was all ready, with his scarf stylishly draped around his neck. Looking at him, she tried to tidy up her hair. I quickly straightened up too and got to the door. Dev saab was chatting with Ma. '*Sab theek hai?* (Is everything all right?) I just came to ask if both of you are comfortable.' The moment we said, 'Yes, Dev saab, all good,' he replied with a quick 'Okay then, see you on the set,' and knocked on the adjacent door to check on the other actors.

I was amazed! Who does that? It was such a warm, personal touch by the charming legend. He didn't have to, but he did, and left his mark on our hearts, leaving us totally floored by this gesture.

When I reached the set, the atmosphere was festive. Jackie Shroff was chilling outside on the bonnet of his car (while waiting for his shot) listening to Dev Anand's songs. Inside, the shot was being set. Dev saab called me to the set to explain what was happening. What I absolutely loved when I noticed it, was that Dev saab, while talking about himself never addressed himself as 'I'. He would always talk about himself in third person. So, while explaining the shot to me, he said, 'So Divya, *Dev ayega, aur kahega* (Dev will come and say) . . .' I was listening intently to this man who was so passionate about his work and so excited about his new film that it was infectious. He was animatedly demonstrating the action that I needed to perform—there was so much energy, so much joie de vivre in it, that I felt lacking in stamina in comparison.

The shoot was so enjoyable that time flew and we didn't realize when it was a wrap for me!

After a few months, I got an invite from Dev saab's office for the premiere of the coloured version of his film *Hum Dono*! How could one even think of missing something so special? My bestie—my Ma—and I reached the venue, super excited. Dev saab was personally welcoming everyone! We were going to watch Dev saab in a double role with the actor himself! The screening started dot on time. Everyone sat mesmerized by the sheer charm and charisma of Dev Anand as the song, *'Main zindagi ka saath nibhata chala gaya'* started playing on the big screen. Everyone in the theatre started cheering, clapping and throwing coins at the big screen! Our very own Jaggu dada (Jackie Shroff) couldn't stop whistling! The atmosphere in the theatre; the magic of Dev Anand and people's love for him was to be seen to be believed. Everyone was celebrating Dev Anand with all their heart!

Dev saab's birthday is a day after mine on 26 September. So, when I wished him, I said in jest, 'Dev saab wish me too, I am a day older than you!'

We met again at the music launch of *Chargesheet.* I was wearing a red dress. As I met Dev saab, he surprised me by saying, 'Red seems to be your favourite colour. When you came to meet me for the first time, you were wearing red at that time too.' That was some sharp memory! Dev saab must be meeting so many people every day and he remembered what a newcomer had worn so many years ago! I was bowled over by him yet again. Of course, I had always been a huge fan but after working with him, I absolutely adored him!

One fine day, I received a call from him. 'Divya, a little issue has come up with the dubbing. Can you come and correct it please?'

'Of course, Dev saab, I will come tomorrow!' I wondered what had gone wrong because when I had dubbed, everything had seemed fine. So, the next day, I reached his studio. He met me warmly and said, '*Wo tumne dialogue mei mujhe dirty old man kaha hai* (You have called me dirty old man in your dialogue) . . .'

I thought he probably wanted me to remove the word 'dirty' but he surprised me again. '*Wo uss line mein se old nikaal do* (take the word old out from that line) . . .'

I was smiling all day. His inimitable spirit had made me fall in love with life and him, all over again.

Love you, Dev saab! They don't make them like you any more.

ADITYA CHOPRA

'You write what you feel like. I trust you,' he said. This is what he wrote back when I messaged him if he'd like to read the chapters on him and Yash ji, once they were written.

These words had an impact on me in a big way. In today's times, it's also a tall order, but I guess trust was the foundation of my journey with this supremely talented, intelligent and ever-dependable filmmaker, whom I actually felt extremely secure with: Aditya Chopra.

I was in London, when I got a call that Aditya Chopra wanted to meet me. My heart began pounding with excitement. *Dilwale Dulhania Le Jayenge* was a cult film, and I was mesmerized by the skilful way in which each emotion of love, drama and thrill was woven into this film for the audience—an absolute treat! The film has been in the theatres for more than twenty-five years, breaking all records. I had always marvelled at the creative sensitivity of this one man, Aditya Chopra. So now, when I got this message, I wondered what he wanted to meet me for. Then my team told me that it was for a film that Aditya was writing, which was to be directed by Yash Chopra. Oh my god! That was a lethal combination! *What could be better than that?*

I grew restless to reach India and meet Adi (as he's fondly called), to know what was in store for me in the film. It was also the first time that I was to meet him in person. As soon as I got back, a meeting was arranged—I was to meet both Yash ji and Adi. My excitement knew no bounds.

I first met Yash ji (about whom I have written in the earlier chapter). My face fell when he broke the news about me being considered to play the heroine's friend. Dreams of me dressed in a chiffon saree, singing on the Alps in a Yash Chopra film had come crashing down.

Just then, Aditya Chopra entered the office. I hadn't said anything, I was still trying to grasp the news. Yash ji said, 'Aditya is the writer, he'll tell you more.'

I was thinking, what more is left to tell—a friend's role, after all, is a friend's role, and our industry is always in a tearing hurry to typecast you with an image, especially if it comes from the biggest banner.

Adi quietly joined in and said a pleasant hi. I was trying to look and sound pleasant too, but somewhere, the excitement of finally having met two of the biggest and finest filmmakers had merged with my disappointment of being relegated to a friend's role. I do not know which expression was finally showing itself on the surface. Whichever it was, the intelligent director had gauged it.

Adi sat and narrated the gist of *Veer-Zaara* to me. It was a dream, this film, and I knew it would be a memorable one. After the narration, I just wanted to get up and clap. Suddenly, I realized, that I was lucky to be sitting in front of these two stalwarts and even listening to the narration (for many, it would probably have just been a dream). Of course, I had loved the narration and really wanted to do *Veer-Zaara*, but the nagging thought of being branded in a friend-type role kept coming back.

I was brought back from my thoughts when Adi said, 'Are you apprehensive?' He had read my mind.

A normal reaction would have been an instant yes to the film, and a yes again and again! Who wouldn't want to be a part of a film directed by Yash Chopra and written by Aditya Chopra, starring Shah Rukh, Amit ji, Preity, Rani, Hema ji? A dream cast by any standards! Only, I'd be a filmi friend.

I managed to mumble, 'I absolutely want to do it but . . .' I couldn't complete it.

'. . . it is not a regular friend's role,' Aditya completed the sentence for me. 'We wouldn't call you for it otherwise. I have written it and it is one of my most favourite roles.'

I was all ears. He continued, 'I can only say one thing. You will always be remembered for playing Shabbo. The rest, of course, is your call . . .' I had been told earlier that Aditya had seen my TV series, *Kadam*, where I'd played different characters in each episode (a delight for an actor), and he was keen on me playing Shabbo.

I sat there looking at him. He had spoken very genuinely and yet in a matter-of-fact manner. There was something about the way he had said it—I felt like jumping into it with full faith and trust. There was a quality about him that made me, as an actor, feel absolutely relaxed. The inner voice said, 'Trust him. Leave it to him na, enjoy the journey!'

That was true. If they wanted, they could have cast someone bigger too, but they had chosen a fairly new person. Yash ji and Adi sat there as I uttered, 'Of course, I trust you and I'd love to do it.' As I said it, my apprehensions flew out of the window and the surge of excitement that had been brewing inside finally came out. I was smiling, and this time, the expression that came up on my face was exactly what was going on inside, that of absolute joy for being able to work with the best.

The journey of preparing for Shabbo turned out to be one of my most cherished experiences. The responsibility of getting me ready for the dialect that Shabbo would speak was taken on by Aditya himself, and my visits to the Yash Raj office started soon after. There were readings galore—Aditya would listen carefully to how I mouthed the beautiful lines written by him. The dialect chosen for me was from a Pakistani province, so once I had mastered the lines and the nuances within them, it was time for me to learn the distinct way to speak those lines.

Nasreen Munni Kabir, a renowned author and a family friend of the Chopras, helped me with that. It was a sing-song way of delivering lines, but I was told that the way they spoke in that manner also varied depending on which strata of society one belonged to. Shabbo was supposed to be the housekeeper.

My most interesting experience was when a call was made to a household in Lahore. Adi told me, 'Listen carefully to how they talk. You shall talk to the lady of the house and the house help. Mark the difference in their styles and remember both.'

I found this process extremely interesting and intriguing too. I listened to the graceful lady's voice on the other side—it was with an accent but the delivery was straight. Then she handed over the phone to the house help. His lines sounded rhythmic and were spoken in a sing-song way—yes, there was a big difference in the way they spoke!

After the phone call, I delivered the lines like the house help, and saw Adi shutting his eyes and listening intently. 'Yes, this works, but let's try a few more variations.' A recording with the house help's voice was organized for me and I worked hard, trying to deliver my dialogues in that dialect. Adi asked me to give him a few variations, and then he shut his eyes again.

The normal psyche, especially for an actor, is that when someone is watching you intently, and is all ears, you increase your efforts, you better your performance, and you deliver better because you are being watched with full attention.

So, I gave it my best. After all, Adi was going to finalize the accent that sounded right for Shabbo. I gave him six different variations altogether. He opened his eyes, clearly decisive. 'The fourth one,' he said. He had actually remembered each rehearsal! I looked at him in awe—that was his focus and passion for his work. He had given his Shabbo a voice now and he seemed pleased (he wouldn't say it, being the reserved guy that he is, but he looked happy for sure). But he said this, 'Good, I think we are on track!'

Shabbo was ready to face the camera for this very special film.

The shooting, of course, was a joy ride. Adi would always hear my rehearsal before my shot and a thumbs up from him was truly uplifting. Being amongst all the biggies and trying to hold your own was a bit overwhelming, but we sailed through well. In between shoot breaks, the crew, along with Adi, would play cricket as a breather and I remember I joined the team with what I knew best, or rather could manage—fielding. On the cricket pitch, I saw a laughing and smiling Aditya and his fun side. That's where I opened up to him.

During the shoot, we would discuss scenes, and have great conversations whenever time permitted. I enjoyed his take on various topics (an absolutely well-read, intelligent man with a natural knack for the artistic, and a mature perspective on life) talking to him was a pleasure.

Veer-Zaara went on to become a big blockbuster, and Aditya Chopra's words turned out to be prophetic. I was loved in the role. I was nominated across all possible awards, and to date, people love me the most for Shabbo. I was surprised with the response, but he knew. He always knew.

During my visits later to the Yash Raj studio, to meet Yash ji,
I would bump into Adi occasionally and end up spending a few
minutes chatting. After a few months, I got a call again from
Yash Raj. This was a comeback film for the lovely Madhuri
Dixit, and Adi asked me to play her friend. But this time, I was
not apprehensive at all about what was being offered—there
was absolute and total trust in the man who sat in front of me
in his huge office. He read my mind again, before I burst into a
smile, and said, 'You have a parallel track, and you are the twist
in the story.'

I didn't ask any further. He continued, 'And I'd like to give
you a happy surprise. When you get to know who we are getting
to play your husband . . .'

I couldn't wait to hear the name. Seeing my curious
expression, he said with a smile, '. . . Irrfan Khan.'

Adi always looked over me. He'd placed me beautifully
in the larger scheme of the film, and somewhere, I loved his
faith in me as an actor. *Aaja Nachle* was a fun shoot for me,
and my role in it was beautiful. The film was directed by Anil
Mehta (the ace cinematographer), and written by Jaideep
Sahni. So, I didn't meet Adi on the sets. But somewhere
within, I was sure that he was always looking over me . . .
and that was reassuring.

After Yash ji passed away, I didn't want to lose this amazing
connect I had with the Yash Raj studio, and I continued my
tea-time visits to Adi's office once in a while, sharing with
him what movies I was working on and, of course, chatting on
various topics over a cup of green tea. One fine day, I took an
appointment to meet Aditya Chopra, little knowing that after
that meeting, I would come back a different person.

As always, I sat in his office, sipping on green tea. He
joined me in a while and we started chatting in general.

He asked me about all the projects that I was working on. Like an exuberant, excited child, I parroted, 'Oh, I've actually signed about a dozen films, so and so with this one, that one with so and so . . .,' and then I paused to take a breath. I was expecting a happy reaction from him. I was sure he would have been extremely happy for me. But there was silence instead. I was confused.

After a long pause, he said softly, 'Divya, why are you in a hurry to do so many films?' I was a bit taken aback. He continued, 'Are you doing them for money?'

I reacted instantly, 'Of course not. Thankfully, I am fine. It just feels so good to be so busy and relevant,' I said.

A pause again and he said, 'You, Divya, are a fantastic actor. Be selective about your films. Leave behind a legacy.'

Those words hit me hard. His voice reverberated in my head, playing up again and again even after I left. He was so right. *What was I doing?* Signing a dozen-odd films, instead of choosing the best and carving a niche for myself. It was going to be my showreel for life, and I had to make sure it was studded beautifully with precious ones rather than anything and everything. I had to build my own position, and his words gave me the strength and assurance that I could.

After that meeting, my perspective towards my work changed. I stopped signing any and every film that came my way. I only took those which had my heart jumping with what I heard, the roles that I really wanted to play, the directors I really wanted to work with. Slowly, but surely, word spread that Divya Dutta 'doesn't take up every role, so find something really exceptional to offer before approaching her'.

Gradually, my films were being talked about, so were my role choices. Most journalists would say, 'If you are in a film, there has to be something special—you choose well.'

I had one man to thank for this.

I had worked hard but this wouldn't have happened without those words. In life, you always need that someone who directs you to the right path, who shows you the way. It is always your own journey, but it's a blessing if someone shows you the path. In my case, I was very fortunate it was Aditya Chopra.

Strangely, I didn't get to meet him after that or tell him this too. But I am sure he knows.

Because he knew. He always knew.

And finally, there are those who have shone bright in my galaxy and it brings me a big smile when I think of them. This book won't be complete without sharing these precious titbits about them.

HRISHIKESH MUKHERJEE

I was sitting at home, trying to make a list of directors I wanted to call to fix meetings for myself. My film, *Train to Pakistan*, had just released, and I thought I could meet people with that reference and procure some good work.

Just then, the landline rang. I picked it up, a bit preoccupied. The voice on the other side was warm, 'Hello,' he said, in a slightly frail voice, '*Divya se baat ho sakti hai?*'

'*Ji, bol rahi hun. Aap kaun?*' I asked in a hurry to hang up and make my calls.

At that moment, I wasn't prepared for what I was going to hear. He continued, '*Hrishikesh Mukherjee bol raha hun.*'

The receiver slipped from my hand. 'What?' *The* Hrishikesh Mukherjee! My most favourite films have been his—*Guddi, Bawarchi, Chupke Chupke, Khubsoorat* and *Gol Maal*. I had always wished to be directed by Hrishi da—I have adored and literally grown on his movies!

And was I talking to him now? Why would he have called me, he probably didn't even know I existed. This surely was a prank call, I concluded. But before I could hang up, my curiosity led me to continue the conversation further. 'Is that Hrishikesh Mukherjee, the director?' I asked, naively.

I could hear a chuckle on the other side. '*Haan beta, main hi hun. Tumhara movie dekha,* Train to Pakistan. *Tumhara kaam bahut accha laga. Main to ab ghar pe hi hota hun, ho sake to aakar milo.*'

That voice was definitely his. It was very genuine and affectionate. I heard myself reply, 'Ji dada, I'll be there tomorrow.' He gave me the address, and I promised to be there. I was still a little doubtful about whether someone was playing a fast one on me, but what if it was actually him? I had to take that chance. If it was true, then I couldn't wait to meet my favourite director.

With mixed feelings, of either being duped or experiencing the happiest moment of my life, I landed at a Bandra house. I could already feel its bright and lovely vibes as I entered. I was ushered in by the house help.

So, it was for real! I was actually at Hrishi da's house! It was actually a phone call from him! He had called me. I was overwhelmed with joy as I was taken to his room.

He was partially lying down, his head resting on the headrest. '*Aaja beta,*' he said affectionately. It was him. I had seen his pictures.

I reverently went and sat on the chair kept next to him. 'How are you, dada? I am so, so happy to meet you.'

He smiled warmly and said, '*Arey, tera film dekha. Bahut pyaari lagi tum film mein, to socha tumko milun.*' I was speechless. The legendary Hrishikesh Mukherjee had wanted to meet me? I was overwhelmed.

'Dada . . .' I whispered and started talking as if I had known him for ever. 'Dada, I have loved all your films. *Aur sab film dekh ke laga,* I wish I was in them, being directed by you. *Kitni sunder filmein!*'

I could go on and on. I thought I would cry in an attempt to express my adulation and love for him and his movies. But I stopped myself in time.

Dada held my hand in his frail hands and said, '*Bees-pachees saal pehle aati na filmon mei, to tere sath bahut filmein banata.*'

That tears that I had tried to control finally fell. 'Dada, you would have worked a lot with me? Really? This means the world to me.' I was trying to absorb what he had said, and the magnanimity of what it meant to me. This, coming from Hrishikesh Mukherjee, was a huge thing for a newcomer like me who was also a huge fangirl.

I sat with him for about an hour, discussing his films, and my background, over a cup of chai. In that one hour, I felt as if I had known him for ever. I was laughing, joking with him and he was indulging me like a child, smiling through it. With a heavy heart, I got up to say goodbye. '*Milte hain jaldi*, dada.' As I said that, I could feel a tug in my heart.

'*Haan beta, apna khayaal rakhna aur achi filmein karna.*'

I never met him after that. He passed away a few months later.

I couldn't deal with his going away—one, because of his films' impact on me, and two, because of this new connect I had formed with him, he felt like my own. I played all his movies one by one, read all his interviews and anecdotes. His smile and laughter kept ringing in my head, and the song too, from his famous film *Anand*: '*Kahin door jab din dhal jaye, sanjh ki dulhan badan churaye, chupke se aye . . .*'

This star is still shining bright in my sky!

DILIP KUMAR

I have literally grown up on his films because my mother was a diehard fan of his. She would swoon over *'Dil Tadap Tadap Ke Kah Raha'*. I started watching his films with Ma, and was bowled over. The romance and depth in those eyes in *Mughal-e-Azam*, and his pranks and vulnerability in *Ram aur Shyam,* all his movies like *Aan, Madhumati* and *Naya Daur* were landmarks in acting, screen presence and nuances. So, I too, share the same sentiments as my mother when it comes to Dilip Kumar.

Once, at a party long back, Ma and I realized that Yusuf saab, as he is fondly called, was there too, with Saira ji. I could see the twinkle in Ma's eyes, and her child-like excitement to meet her most favourite actor. The only hitch was I didn't personally know them, and I was sure they didn't know me at all. Yet, I mustered some courage as I had to fulfil my mother's biggest wish. I made my way through the crowd to reach them. Saira ji was holding Yusuf saab's hand and having a conversation with someone. There was huge security around them, and visitors were not allowed in their proximity.

When I reached them, I introduced myself, *'Adaab Saira ji, adaab* Yusuf saab. I am Divya Dutta, an actor, and my mother

is Yusuf saab's hugest fan. May I get her to meet him, please?'
Saira ji smiled warmly and said, 'Of course, *zaroor*.'

I quickly caught hold of Ma, and introduced her to her
childhood crush. For me, that moment, when I saw Ma's
expressions when she shook hands with Yusuf saab, was
priceless. It will be among my most cherished moments—
seeing Ma's glowing child-like face. Yusuf saab greeted her with
an adaab, and Ma was floored. This little gesture from them left
me overwhelmed and grateful. How much happiness had their
graciousness brought us!

The next time, I met the lovely couple at their house where
I had gone with the editor of a magazine to wish Yusuf saab on
his birthday. Saira ji had been a gracious hostess and Yusuf saab
met everyone warmly, though he wasn't too well.

An incident I'll always remember was at B.R. Chopra ji's
bungalow-cum-studio. I had just done *Baghban* with them, so
they'd invited me to a special screening of the coloured print
of *Naya Daur*. Since it was a Dilip Kumar film, I made sure Ma
accompanied me. Ravi Chopra, the host of the evening, told me
that only a select few people had been invited as Yusuf saab was
coming to watch the film. This was the happiest surprise for Ma
and me. How many people can have the pleasure of watching
a legend's film with the legend himself? It was such an honour!

We took seats in the back. The movie started in a bit.
The coloured version of the superhit film was like the cherry
on the cake. The famous race sequence started, and we could
suddenly hear cheers coming from the front row. We realized
Yusuf saab was clapping and cheering, watching the exciting
sequence on screen. Seeing him, everyone started cheering and
the atmosphere inside the dark theatre was of enthusiasm and
celebration. I sat there in the back seat, truly amazed at the
thespian's love and passion for his craft. He was so engrossed

in it while watching his own sequences, and reminiscing his shooting experiences. His enthusiasm for his craft hadn't reduced one bit. He still felt as passionately about those scenes as he must have when he first shot for them decades ago. That was an inspiration.

I never got an opportunity to work with Dilip Kumar, but his passion and love for cinema did rub off on me that day, and I took one lesson back home along with the most amazing experience of watching *Naya Daur* with Dilip Kumar—love your craft and enjoy the process of it so much that even with time, and under any given circumstances, it remains undeterred and unfazed.

I came home remembering that and humming, 'Maang ke saath tumhara maine maang liya sansar . . .' That saath, the company of this thespian in those few hours, literally meant the world to me.

PREM CHOPRA

Who doesn't know his name? After all, he had said his name in the most popular dialogue ever: '*Prem naam hai mera, Prem Chopra.*' He is among the topmost villains Hindi movies have ever had.

I met him on the sets of *Delhi-6*—tall, pleasant, and very cultured and affable. We didn't really get to interact much there, but much later I realized that he was the father of my very dear friend Punita, who's married to another co-actor and friend of mine, Vikas Bhalla.

We actually bonded well at the Punjabi Star Awards held in Canada, where I had gone with Ma and my brother Rahul. Prem sir was accompanied by his family, including Punita and Vikas.

So, it was a celebration for all of us. Prem sir would take medical advice from Rahul once in a while, and somewhere along the way started trusting him a lot. My exuberant Punjabi mother took no time in befriending him and his wife. After all, Prem sir has Punjabi roots too. So, we all met there pretty often at some dinner or get-together.

One such evening, my mother told Prem sir and his wife, in typical motherly fashion (this was the only point where she would be a typical Ma), '*Suniye, meri beti ke liye bhi accha ladka dhoondiye na* (Listen, please find a good match for my daughter too),' she said, much to my embarrassment. I didn't realize that the Punjabi man to whom this was said had taken the responsibility very seriously.

Before I knew it, my friend Punita called me a few times, saying, 'Dad has fixed for you to meet his friend's son.' I had never been comfortable with an arranged match scenario, but I could never say no to Prem sir. The way he had taken it upon himself to get this 'bacchi' married to a good guy was absolutely endearing. It's a separate issue that those matches didn't work out for me, but what did work out was a beautiful bond with Prem sir. He became like family to us.

He even attended his Doctor saab's (my brother's) wedding. I remember our invites had the wrong time printed so instead of 8 p.m., they said 7 p.m. So, we decided to be at the venue just in case we had guests, even though everyone is usually fashionably late.

So, Rahul and his wife, Shweta, were clicking their album pictures, and I was still getting ready with some of my friends helping me with the finery (women, I tell you).

We saw Prem sir arrive at the venue around 7.45 p.m. I gathered myself up quickly, trying to fix my half-set dress and calling out to the couple in between their posing session to come immediately. Prem ji sure was very amused at the confusion, but he graciously wished the couple and left. Of course, we were very embarrassed at our unpreparedness.

I met him again at some events, and his warmth and affection have always been the same—he is the most thorough gentleman that I have come across. It made me realize how different people are sometimes from their screen images. Someone who I was so scared of as a kid because of his onscreen image, became someone I grew so extremely fond of as a human being.

Always wishing you well, sir. For that little time, you made my mother feel that there was someone looking after her daughter's well-being, and that means a lot to me. Thank you, Prem sir, and as you said famously, 'Kar bhala to ho bhala.' May god bless you, always.

VINOD KHANNA

For me, he was one of the most handsome heroes Hindi movies have ever had. His personality and acting prowess added to his enigma. I found him extremely suave and classy, and his swagger always left me enamoured. My heart broke when he didn't get the heroine in *Qurbani*, and I was transported to another world with the words of the song, *'Tum dena saath mera, o humnawaz . . . '*

We never worked together, neither bumped into each other during movie events. However, life did seem to have a little something in store for us. Once, I was flying back from a shoot in Ahmedabad to Mumbai, and as is my habit, I was on my seat a bit early. I was browsing through my mobile, when I heard a very familiar voice, 'Excuse me, may I?' I looked up and saw that handsome face with the famous cleft. He was chivalrously asking me to remove my bag from his seat, so he could sit. Oh my god! He was my co-passenger. I had just gotten lucky!

I said hello rather brightly as I picked up my purse and then there was silence from both ends. That silence lasted only till the flight took off—only till I could control myself. I had to strike a conversation with him, even if he didn't know me at all! So, I gathered some courage and turned towards him in my most graceful avatar, and said, 'Excuse me, sir. Hi. I am Divya Dutta, an actor too. We've actually never met.'

I was so prepared to get a semi-cold response or a polite acknowledgement. But I was surprised. He turned towards me equally warmly and flashed a lovely smile saying, 'Oh, hi. How are you? Of course, I know you, and yes, we've never met.' I thought that would have been the end of the conversation but it wasn't. I started talking about his film journey and I was delighted that he seemed very comfortable chatting with me.

We discussed so many of his films and anecdotes related to them. It was amazing to hear behind-the-scenes stories from him. We didn't realize when our food was served—the conversation was just getting better. I then asked him about his Osho days and his philosophies. It was heartwarming to see him talk straight from the heart about his deep-rooted thoughts and beliefs. I was learning from this extremely intelligent man and his experiences, and also enjoyed his company thoroughly. How I wish I had at least worked with him once, and I told him so. His response was hearty laughter.

The air hostess announced that we were landing. But I had still not had enough of chatting with Vinod Khanna. I was mesmerized, I was impressed, yet again, this time by Vinod Khanna, the person. He was chivalrous enough to make sure I left before him, wishing me all the best and adding, 'Hope we work together,' before leaving.

That journey of two hours remains embedded in my heart. He was my childhood idol, and I had such a fruitful conversation, titbits from which I imbibe in my life to date.

Thank you, sir, for the pearls of wisdom, for the anecdotes you shared that still bring me a smile, for your movies, and . . . for those precious two hours.

DEEPAK BAHRY

Whenever we visited my uncle Deepak Bahry's house in Mumbai during summer vacations, I was enamoured with the fact that he was a big director in the movies, having made the biggest hits of the 1970s and 1980s like *Tarana*, *Agent Vinod* and *Hum Se Badhkar Kaun*.

When he would return from his shoots in the night, along with his entourage, I used to look forward to sitting with him, along with the other kids of the house, to hear of the day's events. His world of movies mesmerized me.

I remember, when I was four years old, my uncle and aunt took me to Kashmir for the shooting of *Tarana*, where Mithun Chakraborty was playing the lead. When my uncle introduced me to him, he lifted me up in the air, and said, '*Meri heroine banegi?* (Will you be my heroine?)' He, of course, had joked, unaware that the little me was completely taken by film life. I wanted to belong to it too, like my uncle.

Even later, the desire remained as strong, but I could never share this with my uncle, as I was scared that he wouldn't be very comfortable about it (back then, parents were more sceptical about their kids joining movies). Later too, when we attended his film mahurats which were organized on a big scale, starring top-notch stars like Akshay Kumar, Salman Khan and Ajay Devgn, I had the strong urge to tell Ma to tell him that I wanted to do his films too, but we never could manage that. We both couldn't share this with him.

Years later, when I got selected in the Stardust Talent Hunt, after the initial apprehension of his child getting into an unpredictable world, he accepted the fact and I stayed with him for a year before moving out to my own house. But I was always reserved with him. So was he. I wanted to talk a lot with him but couldn't muster enough courage ever somehow.

Then one fine day, my Mama called Ma and said that he was directing an ad film, and he would like me to do it. I have never seen Ma more excited ever. It was her deepest desire that her brother work with her daughter. I was equally excited. After years of wanting this, her wish was finally coming true. Ma warned me. 'You make sure there are no date clashes. I want both of you to work together.'

I smiled seeing Ma so happy, and it was an overwhelming experience being directed by my uncle, on whose sets I had literally grown up! My mother didn't come on the set; she was too emotional about it, but she made sure I gave her a minute-by-minute account. All the people I had seen working with my uncle since childhood were there on the set too. I was their actor now and also their baccha because of which I was fully pampered.

I realized how sensitive and meticulous a director my Mama is, and it was a delight being directed by him. Finally!

Gradually, the ice between him and me broke, and he would specially visit home to talk with me, bringing along the most delicious food that he cooked himself. That awkwardness and hesitation that was attached to my relationship with him had disappeared, giving way to a strong and amazing bond.

Now, we sometimes sit together, discussing all the untold *qissas* and anecdotes I always wanted to hear from him but never could, and enjoying and cherishing all the lovely shoot experiences that are part of his repertoire.

Cheers to you, Mama, and to the introduction you gave me through your films to this amazing world that I now belong to. I am so happy I became an actor, doing something every day that I truly love. I wouldn't have wanted it any other way.

And yes, cheers to many more chat sessions between Mama–Bhanji.

I wouldn't want it any other way either.

ACKNOWLEDGEMENTS

I most definitely cannot end this book without a word of gratitude.

When I penned down the chapters, I was a bit nervous about how they would be received by those they were about. When I was writing each chapter, the memories of each person came flooding back, flowing out of my mind as if it had all happened only yesterday. While I wrote about the experiences with my 'stars', I relived each moment; smiled reminiscing fond memories and felt grateful for knowing these lovely people, and walking a short distance of my beautiful film journey with them. And, more importantly, having them reciprocate my love made me look back with utter joy. Yes, I have been very lucky to have them in my life!

I have penned it down with all my heart.

Sometimes, we don't really get to tell the people who mean a lot to us what we really feel about them. The words written for them did that for me. This book made me lay bare all my feelings for them. But what I wasn't prepared for was the magnitude of love coming my way when I shared the chapters with them.

I must mention Aditya Chopra here! When I sent him a message that I was writing chapters on him and Yash ji, his response stumped me! He just wrote back, 'Please write and, you don't need to share either. I totally trust you!' I sat reading that message for very long. I must have earned this trust and that was a huge moment for me.

To some, I e-mailed the chapters. What I received was an instant phone call in voices laden with emotion. We happily discussed all the incidents mentioned, remembering them together and laughing away, moist-eyed . . . strengthening the bond a little more.

To some, I read the chapters out personally and what an experience it was! After the chapter was read, what always followed was silence. I saw them sit quietly, extremely moved. And that overwhelmed me with emotion too. I saw them all feel what I felt—I saw that happy tear trickling out, and for me, that is the treasure I earned . . . of love, of a journey absolutely gratifying . . . each moment with these lovely people etched in my heart.

A big thank you to my brother Rahul and sister-in-law Shweta for being my sounding boards. They were the first ones to hear the chapters and give me their honest feedback. Wherever they were, whatever they were doing, I'd pull them out to sit and listen immediately as I was too curious for their honest reactions. I'll cherish our discussions, after every chapter reading!

A big thank you to my adorable nephew Vehaant and niece Tishya who taught me that heartfelt writing doesn't necessarily need secluded places and silence. I could do it beautifully with their fun and frolic around me . . . with all their masti . . . making me feel alive in the silence of the lockdown.

And to my baby Sakhi, for her serene, soothing and reassuring presence—quietly sitting at my feet and giving me company as I went through various emotions penning this book.

A big thank you to my editor Vaishali Mathur for always believing in me. It's such a relief to know that your editor understands you inside out; lets you flow and stands like a rock, supporting you.

Last, but surely not the least, my Ma. I know you sat with me when I wrote, when I was nervous sharing the chapters with the stars, and when I jumped all around the house like a baby after I'd received their unexpected reactions. You sat there watching me and smiling at your *baccha* and her exuberance.

I felt you with me each time.

I look back and feel blessed. Of all that I have achieved, the biggest earning has been the love from my family, friends and the world I love the most—my film world—and the beautiful people that belong to it. I just can't thank you all enough. You all shine bright in my life.

You are the stars in my sky.